Fashionably Late

Gay, Bi & Trans Men Who Came Out Later in Life

Fashionably Late

Gay, Bi & Trans Men Who Came Out Later in Life

edited by

Vinnie Kinsella

Eldredge Books
PORTLAND, OREGON

For all those still in hiding.

Acknowledgments

When I started listing people to include in the acknowledgments, I began with those you'd likely expect me, as the anthology's editor, to thank: friends who encouraged me to move forward with the project when I first conceived of it, supportive colleagues in the publishing industry, early backers of the project, the proofreaders, the cover designer. All of these people deserve my thanks, and all of them have it. But as I thought about who else helped make this book possible, it dawned on me that the people who deserve the most thanks are people I've never met. I am referring to the many brave people who fought for LGBTQ equality long before I was born and all during the years that I was closeted and too afraid to fight for myself.

Although LGBTQ people today experience a higher level of acceptance from mainstream society than ever before, I am reminded that not too long ago, police routinely raided bars that catered to gays and lesbians, California's first openly gay politician was assassinated shortly after taking office, and those dying of AIDS were left to fend for themselves when the government turned a blind eye to their suffering. I am also reminded that rioters pushed back against police harassment at the Stonewall Inn, that Harvey Milk's death amplified his message that change will happen when we no longer hide ourselves from the world, and that the government's refusal to help the sick and vulnerable did not go unchallenged. Many out and proud baby boomers and Gen Xers fought hard for a future they believed in, a future where no one had to hide their sexual or gender identities to serve in the military, where legal marriage was no longer the privilege solely of straight people, and where the health and well-being of sexual and gender minorities wasn't threatened on a daily basis. They fought for the generations to come, but did they know they were also fighting for their closeted peers?

When I speak with men who came out later in life, I often hear them say they did so because they realized how much the world had changed since they were young. That change didn't happen on its own. It took many battles. It's the brave fighters who fought these battles I most want to thank here at the start of this book. Without your courage leading the way, many of the men whose stories are featured in this book might have gone to the grave still closeted. When people read this book, I hope they see it as I do: a testament to how you changed society. May you take pride in knowing that your bravery opened doors of hope for both the future *and* the present.

Vinnie Kinsella,
Editor

Contents

Living La Vida Media 199

Reid Vanderburgh

Today, anyone who meets Reid would never guess he was assigned female at birth. But did his transition make him a man? In this essay, he ponders what it means to transition from female to not-female.

Cellophane 203

Joseph A. Shapiro

While enjoying a night of song at an iconic New York gay bar, Joseph spots a younger man reminiscent of himself. The experience brings to mind memories of evenings spent with his former wife.

Introduction

Vinnie Kinsella

"WHO IS THE FIRST PERSON YOU CAME OUT TO?"

It was a seemingly straightforward question, one most men surrounding me in the circle didn't need to think long about before answering: "My ex-wife was the first person I came out to." "My mom." "My sister." "My son."

Although we varied in socioeconomic backgrounds, religious beliefs, and generational labels, these men and I held one thing in common: we came out of the closet later in life. We were gathered inside the boardroom of our local HIV testing center for our monthly PDX Late Bloomers Club discussion group.[1] It was our time to talk with one another about the struggles and joys we'd experienced coming out. As is our norm, we started our meeting with an icebreaker question as a way to introduce new members to the group. As the facilitator of the discussion, I usually come up with these questions. But this question—who is the first person you came out to?—didn't come from me. It came from one of the regular attendees.

With no answer immediately coming to my mind, I decided to exercise my facilitator privilege by insisting we start with the man on my left and go clockwise around the circle. With over twenty men in attendance that day, I would have plenty of time to come up with my answer. But as we went around the circle and the men began to rattle

---

1. PDX is the airport code for Portland, Oregon. Locals use it as an abbreviation for the city.

off their answers, I found it increasingly difficult to pinpoint just who that first person was for me.

There were many people from my religious days who knew I desired to rid myself of my same-sex attractions: pastors who'd counseled me, close friends I'd confided in, exorcists who'd sought to cast the demon of homosexuality out of my life (yes, I actually tried that). But since they were let in on the secret in order to help keep me from acting on my attractions, did any of them count? What about the first man I ever chatted with through a gay dating app? Did it count as me coming out to him if he assumed I was gay from the start? What about the friend I spilled my heart out to one night in a teahouse after I realized my many attempts to become straight were never going to pay off? I suppose that might have counted, but that still didn't feel like the correct answer. The fact was, I struggled to come up with an answer because I wasn't exactly sure when I officially came out. I just knew that sometime between my thirty-fourth and thirty-fifth birthdays, I went from being a man who struggled with unwanted same-sex attractions to being a man who no longer saw those attractions as anything to struggle against—a man who no longer kept being gay a secret.

As it turns out, defining what it means to come out is not that simple. Although LGBTQ people agree that coming out of the closet is something a person either has or has not done, we don't always agree on where the line between "has done" and "has not done" is drawn. For some, telling just one other person that you are somehow other than the assumed sexual or gender norm qualifies as being out. To others, you're not really out until you make your otherness known publicly. For others still, it comes by degrees, such as being out to friends and family but not to coworkers. Understood in all of the definitions, however, is the idea that coming out is more than just an event—it's a process we must choose to maintain if we want to avoid "going back in."

When I first started intentionally socializing with other LGBTQ people (something I had avoided easily beforehand by filling up my free time with church functions), I often heard them say, "Coming out is a lifestyle. You will always be coming out." I didn't know what that meant. To my way of thinking, coming out ended when I reached the point where I was no longer keeping my gayness hidden from the people I cared about. What I didn't consider was that life would continue on after that point and I would meet new people. Each party I attend, each new work relationship I forge, provides me with a chance to either disclose my sexuality or keep it under wraps. Sometimes, making my sexuality known doesn't matter. If I am having dinner with a female friend and the server assumes we're on a date, what do I care? Sometimes, it matters a great deal. If I join a new social organization that claims to be open to everyone, I test that claim right away by letting the members know I'm gay. As I've learned, it's one thing for a group to make a claim of inclusivity but another thing entirely to put that claim into practice. It is this ongoing need to choose when and where to disclose my sexuality that turns coming out into a lifestyle.

I also learned from others in the LGBTQ community that being out can have multiple meanings. For my transgender friends who have transitioned and appear as cisgender to the public, coming out is no longer about announcing a transition—it's about choosing whether or not to disclose that their transitions took place.[2] For my bisexual friends, coming out can be more about visibility than letting others know they are attracted to both men and women. For those of them in committed relationships with a member of the opposite sex, coming out is about combating the notion that bisexuality isn't a valid sexual identity. It's their way of saying, "I might be in a heterosexual relationship, but that does not make me heterosexual."

Given the nuances of what it means to be out, perhaps it is easy to see why I was having a difficult time figuring out when that exact

---

2. For those confused by terminology, *transgender* is an umbrella term generally referring to people whose gender identities don't align with their biological sex. *Cisgender* is a term for people whose gender identities do align with their biological sex. It's import to note that not all transgender people desire to appear cisgender, and some do not have the means to do so even if they want to.

moment between being in and being out took place for me. And I wasn't the only man in the circle pondering this.

"Which time?" one man asked, causing several others to laugh. His was a story common among those in my group. It was one of a man who began coming out as gay in his early twenties but reversed direction to marry a woman, delaying his coming out for another twenty-plus years. It was a story I personally couldn't relate to, having never been married, but I still empathized with. It was a path I tried to go down.

I had attempted dating women in my twenties and early thirties with the intent to marry, somehow believing that marriage would rid me of my sexual attraction to men and instill in me a sexual attraction to women that had never been there before. These relationships never got far. This was largely due to the fact that I had in mind that the woman for me would be the one I actually wanted to have sex with. When I found her, I would marry her. Unsurprisingly, no woman was ever able to elicit that response in me.

Ironically, it was a seemingly sure-shot chance at marriage to a woman that pushed me out of the closet. One evening, without warning, a platonic female church friend of twelve years expressed her interest in dating me, citing the longevity of our friendship as a good reason for us to give it a go. She was in her early thirties, had never been married, and for that matter, had never really dated. She was eager to end her days as a single woman (something often stigmatized in religious circles where gender roles are strongly defined). I knew that she was looking at me as low-hanging fruit: a decent thirty-four-year-old unattached man she already knew she could get along with. But what had made our friendship work for me was the fact that there was no hope of romance between us. I assumed she harbored unspoken same-sex attractions like I did, making it easy for me to relate to her without worrying there would be pressure to date. In my mind, we were two closeted queer people who had bonded over an unspoken understanding of one another's struggles to live by heteronormative standards. Her declaration of interest shocked me.

Given her pressing desire to marry, I knew saying yes to her advances would lead to us walking down the aisle—and I just couldn't do it. At thirty-four, I had experienced enough failure at becoming straight to know that marriage wasn't strong enough to rid me of my attraction to men, that I would have to lie about who I was for the rest of my life. As I thought about how much work would go into maintaining that lie, I decided it was time to cut my losses. I let go of all the worthless pastoral counseling I'd received on how to make myself desire women and chucked all the garbage books I'd read by ex-gay ministers claiming to have experienced deliverance from homosexuality (many of these men now identify as ex-ex-gays). Nothing could ever really change me. By letting it all go, I ruffled a lot of religious feathers, lost a lot of friends, and had to leave behind the comfort of a familiar yet intolerant religious community in order live as an openly gay man.

Moving forward was a lonely experience at first. When it came to integrating into the gay community, I felt behind by at least a decade, making it difficult for me to find a place to fit in. Most out men my age knew the ropes, knew the cultural norms, and didn't have a lot of patience for someone who was learning what they had figured out fifteen to twenty years prior. In my attempts to integrate into gay culture, there were a lot of awkward moments. But as time moved on, I began to enjoy exploring my new community and found myself feeling more like an insider and less like an interloper.

As I connected with more gay men, I found a few others who had come out after the age of thirty. I even dated one of them for a short while. As immature as that relationship was, I enjoyed having someone in my life who understood what it was like to experience the world anew as an adult, someone who had patience for my ignorance because he too was figuring out what it meant to be gay. I often joked that we should start a group for men like us. When that relationship fizzled out, I turned that joke into a reality by logging on to Meetup.com and creating the PDX Late Bloomers Club for gay, bi, and trans men.

I hoped to find about eight to ten other out-late guys to spend time with. I had no idea what I was starting.

In just a few months' time, over one hundred men joined the Meetup group, several of which were still in the closet. It turns out that in putting up a virtual sign that read, "I am looking for others like me," I provided a rallying point for a segment of the population no one knew needed a rallying point. Before long, my social group had to adapt. Instead of a group with a few guys who got together to eat dinner or go to a show, we became a social-support group with both a monthly discussion group meeting and occasional social events.

Our monthly discussion groups regularly draw in new men looking for support and affirmation. We offer no formal plan for coming out, no twelve-step program for recovering from a life spent in hiding. Instead, we just gather and talk. Some men ask burning questions of the group: "If you were married, how did your wife take the news?" "How long did you wait to disclose to men you were dating that you have kids?" Other men offer their experiences in response: "My wife left me." "My wife and I are still married. We just have an open marriage now." "I get the kid thing out of the way as soon as I can. I can't date someone who won't want my kids in his life."

If the conversation doesn't go deep, it doesn't really matter. What matters is that men come in feeling isolated in their identities as late bloomers and leave knowing there are many others like them.

At the meeting when I pondered how to answer the question of who I first came out to, I was the youngest in attendance. This is not uncommon, as the group tends to be made up of baby boomers and Gen Xers. Our diversity in age has led to some discussion about who, exactly, qualifies as a late bloomer. Being born in 1978, I butt up against the line between Generation X and the millennial generation. When I say I came out of the closet at thirty-four, millennials ask what took me so long. Baby boomers congratulate me on getting it done while I still have so much life ahead of me. In the same way that the line between being in the closet and being out of the closet is relative to the one defining what it means to be out, what it means to come out late is also relative. I know men who came out in their late sixties and men who came out in their midtwenties who equally feel they did it late. And I have no right to tell either they are wrong for feeling that way. The truth of the matter is that there is no agreed-upon age after which one is considered to have come out late. Such an agreement would imply that coming out is some sort of age-based rite of passage, like getting your driver's license at sixteen.

Regardless of how coming out late is defined, I knew two things as I sat in that circle that day: I had indeed come out, and I wished I had done it much sooner. But I realized there was no way I could have come out sooner than I did. I wasn't ready to open up about my sexuality to others earlier because I hadn't yet accepted for myself the fact that I was gay. It was in realizing this that I found my answer.

The first person I came out to was me.

My first true act of coming out, the moment I crossed the line from being in the closet to being out of the closet, was the day I faced myself in the mirror and said the words, "I am gay."

When I gave my answer, many of the men in the circle nodded in understanding. They all understood that no matter how you define coming out, self-acceptance is what opens the closet door. When we are able to reject the voices that tell us we should be ashamed of our otherness and instead embrace who we are without judgment, the opinions of others lose their power. Each time we assert to ourselves that there is nothing wrong with who we are, it becomes that much easier to set aside the affected straight or cisgender identities we hid behind. Yes, we might suffer the loss of friends and family who refuse to accept us when the masquerade ends, but we gain something in return. We gain the ability to love ourselves.

Reaching that moment when we are able to come out to ourselves is often the hardest part of the process. I have seen many men who attend our monthly Late Bloomer meetings on the cusp of this moment. They come not quite sure if they are ready to own who they are. They come seeking assurance that if they do accept themselves and come out, it won't be the end of the world. For such men, walking into a room filled with others who have taken that first step out of the closet and kept on walking often fills them with courage. They see that there is a life for them out in the open, and that it's never too late to live it. I love watching as that realization hits a closeted man and gives him the last boost of courage he needs to move forward. I also love watching as members of the group provide peer support that older men often don't have when coming out.

In thinking about what a wonderful experience the PDX Late Bloomers Club offers, I began to think about men who don't have such an organization near them. How can they find a circle of their own to sit in? Better yet, how can I offer them such an experience? I found the answer in my career in book publishing. As someone who has spent most of his adult life helping others publish books, I know the unique power an anthology has to connect geographically disparate people with shared identities. With that knowledge in mind, I set myself to work on *Fashionably Late*.

Each man featured in this anthology forged his own path out of the closet, and none of the paths were smooth. Yet each man made it out. And now, out in the open, they offer their stories in the hope of affirming others like them.[3] I acknowledge the bravery of each man featured in these pages. They are not opening up about their lives in a small circle behind closed doors. Instead, they are opening up in a circle that the whole world can sit in on. For some of the authors featured

---

3. Although the target audience for this book is late-blooming gay, bi, and trans men, I hope it also finds its way into the hands of those who love these men and seek to better understand them. Perhaps the wife whose husband of thirty years is just now telling her he's gay or bi will find insight in these pages into why he kept her in the dark for so long. Perhaps the son whose mother has announced she is transitioning to male will get a glimpse into who this new man in his life will be. There in no denying that a man's choice to come out impacts everyone in his life, and many of the stories in this anthology address that reality head-on.

here, including their names in this book is another coming out. This time, not to a friend at a coffee shop or to a trusted colleague at work but to any stranger who picks up this book. These men have chosen to share their stories with you, dear reader, hoping you will find something of yourself in their stories. I know I speak for them all when I say to you, "Pull up a chair and join the circle."

Snow Fell Out of Darkness

Van Waffle

My family's sense of morality came from literature: Tolstoy, Shakespeare, the classics. We didn't swear, go to church, or use rude words like *nigger* or *faggot*. At dinner my mother or I would recount the adventures of Nicholas Nickleby, or Charles Darwin and the Beagle.

Alone in my room, I escaped to approved alternate worlds like Narnia, Earthsea, Middle-Earth, and Camelot. My knowledge of the real world also came from books. I was in my mid-teens in the late 1970s when David Wallechinsky's *The Book of Lists* identified famous people who were gay or lesbian. It helped identify some unruly, forbidden desires I had begun to feel. Unfortunately, Oscar Wilde and Virginia Woolf didn't belong on the shelves of my parents' library.

I attended a high school with five hundred students in a small Ontario town. One day in grade 11 a bunch of kids in my class started saying, "Boing! Boing!" I didn't understand the joke but went along. When I said it, they laughed even harder. For an hour or so, I enjoyed the novelty of making people laugh.

Later, on the way home on the school bus, my neighbor informed me the kids were calling *me* Boing. Someone had noticed me getting an erection in the shower with other boys after gym class. I didn't remember it happening. It couldn't have. I convinced myself it hadn't.

Passing me in the hall, younger kids I didn't know would say, "Boing! Boing!" I pretended not to notice. I learned how to put a brave face on secret despair. Time passed, and the teasing stopped. I had won.

Books didn't give me a word for the hopelessness and isolation I felt. Not until much later in life would I recognize I had depression.

Besides *The Book of Lists*, popular culture offered only scarce hints about gay people, and even then they were usually creepy, lonely people doing unspeakable acts in dark alleys. I had no role model for love except the kind that belonged in families with nice houses and good neighbors. I wanted a family of my own someday more than anything else. The only way I knew to achieve that dream was by getting married the traditional way.

I started attending an Anglican church with some school friends. We arranged music to perform together, and my parents attended our Christmas concert. This was my first experience with religion, and it felt like belonging.

By the last year of high school, my secret had become unbearable. Not long after my eighteenth birthday, I started trying to work it out explicitly in my diary. Believing depression was an inextricable part of my unnatural sexual attraction, I rolled them together as one, calling it by a codename: my inner blackness.

My family was not religious, but I believed in life after death and some kind of all-powerful creator being. Something had made me this way. What terrible thing had I done to deserve this ghastly verdict? What a small thing it seemed: to ask only to be a normal person.

At the same time, I hated myself for being this way. I couldn't stand to go through a whole lifetime with my inner blackness, but the idea of ending my life repulsed me. I thought there were two unforgiveable acts: to kill another person and to commit suicide.

April 19, 1982. I would end my miserable and futile existence if for an instant I believed that death would not be worse. I sense that if I can somehow endure this agony, then I'll at last find repose in death, but if I take my own life, then death will be nothing more than eternal agony. I can only try to live each day as it comes.

April 22. What is this haunting spirit that has entered me now? It is something cold, something listless, far beyond anguish, far beyond anger. This is the most frightening sensation I've ever felt. I must talk to someone before I kill myself.

I became infatuated with my best friend. Sometimes at night I would drive past his house just to be near him, though I would never dream of revealing my feelings.

May 30. I would never lower myself to the loathsome idea of actually, physically loving a man. So it seems I shall live a life of reckless frustrations.

When high school ended, I was both lonely and relieved to have the summer to myself.

June 25. I must see very little of my friend. He causes me more pain than any enemy ever could or would. In spite of my oath never to physically love a man, those physical drives cause relentless anguish.

Soon after starting university in September, I began dating a female art student in her third year who lived in the same dorm. I had made a compromise between what I felt and wanted, persuading myself I was bisexual. One evening I told her. She seemed to accept it, and I was giddy with hope.

Then I didn't see or hear from her for a few days. Finally she left a note saying she couldn't see me anymore. There was nothing wrong with me, she insisted, but she couldn't handle feeling jealous about both women and men. She enclosed a clipping from the campus newspaper, advertising a Halloween dance hosted by the gay student club. I threw out the clipping in disgust and didn't answer her letter, and she drifted out of my life.

One morning during the Christmas holidays, I went into my parents' bedroom and sat beside them on the edge of the bed, crying. Alternating between tears and paralysis, I divulged that I was bisexual. They spent the rest of the day sitting and listening to me.

They didn't reject me. They revealed that a relative in their generation was gay, so it wasn't completely foreign to them. Mom said she had guessed something might be wrong, but didn't know what.

"We only want you to be happy," she declared with resignation.

This shocked me: their belief that I could be attracted to men and be happy. It didn't make sense. I wanted my parents to fix the problem by sending me to a doctor.

Many years later, when I recognized my lifelong ordeal with depression, I discovered mental health problems were harder for my parents to understand or accept. In their generation people often took to alcohol, or sometimes got locked away or hospitalized with vague diagnoses. For them depression was a step toward craziness, more of a secret shame than my sexuality. At age nineteen if I had happily brought home a boyfriend, they probably would have made do.

Being miserable and being gay were the same thing in my mind. Failing to get help from my parents, I didn't speak to them about it for the next few years. They never asked.

At university I found a comfortable social circle. We sat in the common room talking late into the night and went drinking once or twice a week. They were fun but not too wild for a straitlaced boy like me.

A friend asked me to go see *Flashdance* with him. I enjoyed the movie but was too naïve to understand the significance of our date. I had no idea about any kind of gay culture. I liked dancing but hated bands like Culture Club and Eurythmics that blurred gender lines.

In biology lectures I often sat with another guy who talked about Jesus a lot. Although I'd dabbled in going to church, this was my first encounter with faith as an act of commitment. I realized faith was far different from the comfort of making music with friends to play in church—that it could be radical, active, and life changing.

After first year I got a summer job back home. In August I had a few days alone while my parents were away at the cottage. Now nineteen, I could walk into a variety store and buy pornography. One night I drove to another town half an hour away and purchased the latest copies of *Playboy* and *Playgirl*.

The female centerfold was beautiful, but most of the naked women repulsed me. I would never again waste money on a girlie magazine. It started to become clear that I was more gay than bisexual. Whenever I bought one of those magazines, it felt like something else had taken control of my mind and body. I had no choice. The future had never seemed so bleak.

At the same time, I had begun referring to a red pocket Bible I'd been given in elementary school. The front pages suggested some verses to read for help when anxiety, friends' failures, temptation, or other kinds of trouble threatened. These had been particularly useful. One night I happened to flip to the back cover and found for the first time the sinner's prayer, in which a lost soul could find salvation by asking Jesus Christ into his or her life. Its words changed my essential understanding of the universe: how everyone is a sinner and deserves to die, but Jesus died to take away our sins.

This was perfect. It confirmed my belief that the world was a sad and dingy place, that some flaw of nature had determined that I should suffer. If only I resisted the pull of evil until I died, everything would be fine. I needed someone to take away my problems, and in my room that humid August night, God felt suddenly close and capable. I prayed and asked Jesus into my life.

Back at university I contacted a group that held church services on campus every Sunday morning, with Bible studies and prayer meetings throughout the week. The people had great warmth and sense of purpose. They hugged one another easily—men and women, even men and men. It was refreshing. We sang a lot. I especially enjoyed the Sunday-evening breaking of bread, when we sat together quietly reflecting, requesting songs, and sharing personal insights.

Every morning I read my Bible and prayed.

People's openness about their struggles with sin encouraged me to talk about my own. The first time I confided in a friend that I was gay, he reacted with anger.

"Homosexuality is sin, and sin is all it is," he declared.

At first I was humiliated, but later that evening I took comfort in the simplicity of his response. God must have the same view of my feelings. If they were simply a sin, He could take them away.

One night after a swim at the athletic centre, a man caught my eye in the showers. I'd been slipping glances for years, but no one had ever caught me looking. I turned away, but he followed and watched while I dressed. Suppressing curiosity, I hurried out of the locker room, only to wait in the hall, pretending to look at some sign-up sheets on the bulletin board until he caught up. He tried to start a conversation, but I pretended to ignore him, fixing my eyes on the wall. He hung around. I waited. After a while, he left the building. I waited another ten minutes to make sure he was gone, then went outside. He was waiting by the corner of the building in the dark. I had never felt such an irresistible pull, but I turned once more and walked in the other direction. Again, he caught up to me.

"What's your name?" I asked.

"Chuck," he said. "How old are you?"

"Nineteen. How old are you?"

"Too old," he said. He looked in his late twenties.

"Are you married?" I asked.

"Yes."

I continued walking, but he kept pace.

"Do you have somewhere we can go?" he asked.

I just wanted to talk to him. "Want to go for a drink?" I replied.

"It's Sunday evening," he pointed out. "Everything on campus is closed."

We could only be meeting for one reason. I had roommates, so taking him to my residence was not an option. But a rush came over me.

"I have a car," I offered.

We went there, and he guided me to a deserted country road. I parked on the shoulder.

"All power on!" he said.

The steering wheel got in the way, so I suggested moving to the backseat. We did, then started to unbutton and unzip. He had his jeans and underwear around his knees.

Then some headlights flashed in the distance. He flinched. He froze. He didn't move.

"What's the matter?" I asked.

"Someone will find us."

A vehicle whizzed past, shaking the car. I didn't care. My body wanted to take in his body. More than that, I wanted his company and affection. But he remained motionless.

Finally he said, "This wasn't such a good idea."

I drove him back to campus, and we said goodnight. By the next day, I was shaken with remorse. I'd given away my innocence for nothing: no connection, no pleasure, no release. I was lonelier than ever. That would be my last attempt at sex with a man for many years.

I confessed the whole story to my Christian classmate the next day. He responded with more encouragement than expected.

"This won't hurt our friendship," he reassured me. "The Bible says we should confess our sins to one another and pray for one another, because the prayer of a righteous person is powerful. This will make our friendship stronger."

A stronger friendship was what I craved most. His words filled me with hope, but our friendship hardly changed. If anything, we began drifting apart.

We all had our weaknesses, whether it was the temptation to gossip or smoke. After I admitted my problem to another friend, she told me about her abortion some years earlier and how it had scarred her life. Confessions led to emotional intimacy, though more often with women than men. For guys the big problems were usually lust and masturbation; hardly anybody liked talking about those.

My sin was epic by comparison. It made me different. The church elders encouraged me to believe I would one day find fulfillment in godly marriage to a woman. I set my heart on that path.

Church life was not primarily concerned with our own sins, of course. We believed our purpose on Earth was to convert as many people as possible to Christianity before Jesus returned. We had a motto: "Every nation in our generation." Our church had an active ministry at the university. We regularly preached on campus and invited people to Bible studies and Sunday-morning services. Some of the men preached in public. I never did, but I helped hand out gospel tracts and spoke to strangers. One of our tracts was titled "Enjoy Life Now. Ask Me How."

One Sunday evening, the church elders called a special meeting. As we gathered in a room at the university centre, some people entered with grim expressions. When the pastor stood, silence fell. He said a woman in the church had admitted to being a homosexual. She was unrepentant, which meant she refused to renounce her sin. The elders had decided to discipline her according to some verses from the New Testament. Until she agreed to change her ways and ask God for forgiveness, she would be unwelcome in our church. Unless she chose to approach one of the elders, no one was permitted to have any contact with her ever. That same evening, two students were also formally ostracized in the same way for having premarital sex. They were a couple engaged to be married.

I was shocked and sad that these people had given up our church for a life of sin—and scared because these events had struck close to my own weakness. In the next few days, I expressed my fear to the pastor and several friends. Everyone reassured me that I had chosen the right path. They and God were on my side.

This event brought consequences for the church. Nowadays something probably would have happened much sooner, but this was 1987. Someone complained to the university about the church ostracizing people. The administration and chaplains had policies against discrimination on the basis of sexual orientation. The following year our church got kicked off campus. We were no longer permitted to operate as a club or hold meetings there. This disappointed us, but the New Testament gave assurance that strong faith would be met with resistance. We took courage in acting righteously for God.

I spent the next few years getting through school and growing closer to Jesus. I lived in households with other young Christian men. We prayed, ate meals, talked about our lives, and attended church together. I could acknowledge my sexual orientation and, to their credit, none of these friends showed any fear. They treated me like anyone else. In this atmosphere of intimacy with other men, I was happy.

However, I would become infatuated with my closest friends. I even shared a bedroom with one for a few months. He was warm, affectionate, and funny, and he loved me fraternally. I never took advantage of his kindness, but at night I would lie listening to his breathing, hormones carrying me to a drugged state. I thought nothing more wonderful could happen, but in hindsight it was agonizing.

Occasionally when alone, I had the irresistible compulsion to buy pornography. Sometimes when traveling I would take the opportunity to stop in places where no one knew me. If I did buy any magazines, sometimes I would pull off the highway in guilt to heave them into a dumpster without even opening them.

Some American church friends gave me information sheets about an organization for Christians wanting to turn away from homosexuality called Exodus International. So I discovered the ex-gay movement. I wasn't an unusual case, after all. There were thousands of Christians like me, who had experienced homosexuality and found healing through Jesus Christ. Many of them had been sexually active, even living in gay relationships before finding redemption.

Several from a Toronto organization called New Directions came to our city and gave a seminar. Various churches across town sent small delegations. This was unusual, because normally our church did not associate much with other congregations. We were hard-core Bible believers. But on this topic, many were still openly united in the 1980s: Catholics, Presbyterians, Pentecostals, the Salvation Army, and others.

After the presentation, I had a chance to tell my story to one of the guest speakers. He listened, then asked whether my father had been absent or aloof, and whether my mother had been over-involved in my life. These were the classic environmental causes that make a man gay, he said.

I wouldn't necessarily have described my parents in these terms, but my relationship with my mother was close. The ex-gay movement encouraged us to understand ourselves this way. Sin could arise from social problems, such as parents acting outside their appropriate roles. I loved my parents and was a bit uncomfortable with this interpretation of my family, but in time it started to make sense. In complex relationships, almost any pattern will manifest if you think about it long enough.

For the first time, I could talk to people who related to my struggle. They understood how it felt to be attracted to other men, how it sometimes threatened to take over my life.

My life had taken an upturn. I was soon engaged to be married to a woman. She was a member of the same church, and we had been friends for several years. She knew my story and expressed support. My own dream was coming true. I loved her in the way the church taught I ought to love her: as a sister.

By then I had graduated from university, gone to college for journalism, and begun working for a small magazine company. Jayne, the assistant editor, became a good friend. I broke the news to her about my engagement and also admitted my struggle with homosexuality. She was one of the few people outside the church whom I had told.

"Think carefully about this," she warned. "Getting married might not be the right thing for you."

I didn't know what she meant—I didn't want to know. It didn't deter me. I was exhilarated about getting married.

The magazine company folded, and I lost contact with Jayne. I had to move away to get work as a reporter at a rural newspaper. It was hard leaving the church that had nourished me as a young Christian. However, a friend told me about a similar church where I was moving. I quickly found new friends there to confide in.

For the first time, I was living alone instead of in a household with other young Christian men. The nights were quiet and dark, and a long, empty highway ran past my door. With loneliness came a new wave of depression. At the same time, I could sit under the silent night sky, see all the stars, and contemplate my place in creation. Happiness seemed far from reach, and yet when I was most unhappy, I felt closest to God. This didn't fit with the tracts we used to hand out on campus, "Enjoy Life Now. Ask Me How." But my relationship with God seemed to be the only thing saving me from a life of depravity.

A few months after I moved, my fiancée came to live with a retired couple on a farm nearby. This eased my loneliness, but not completely. One evening after dinner, I was watching the sunset with her when a wave of dread came over me. For a moment it seemed like I was making the worst mistake of my whole life. I tried to put these thoughts into words, but she reassured me that all would be well.

"I know your sexuality will come up at times during our marriage," she said.

The panic passed. I was excited in the weeks leading up to our wedding. We were married on a clear, sharply cold day in October. We traveled to Virginia for our honeymoon, and I fell amazingly in love with my wife. A few months later, I got a new job allowing us to move back to the city and our home church. Our first year of marriage seemed happier than anything I had known before.

She had family troubles of her own, quite different from mine. The church had encouraged us to believe that a Christian marriage would help heal both of us. But in hindsight, the people around us were ignorant about unhappiness and in suggesting that a faith-based marriage would help us heal.

My parents' relationship was remarkably happy and stable. I took it for granted that my marriage would be stable too. With the additional help of God, which my parents lacked, surely nothing could go wrong. I thrived on this certainty.

We had two daughters two years apart. This was the fulfillment of my lifelong dream.

But my wife and I had vastly different expectations. I craved a depth of closeness and intimacy that made her uncomfortable.

"It's like a bottomless well," she once said.

What she really wanted, I never knew. We mystified one another. I was a gay man in love with a woman, and she disliked much of my attention. After a brief reprieve, my bouts of loneliness and depression returned.

We had been married fourteen months when our first daughter was born by cesarean section. The nights my wife spent in the hospital, I found it especially hard to go home alone. As my happiness began inexplicably to collapse, I sought help from the ex-gay ministry in Toronto, New Directions.

I placed the first call from my office at work. I had barely introduced myself to the man on the other end of the line when I broke down in tears. To my relief, we arranged a meeting the following day. I got permission to leave work early to meet the counselor.

I was twenty-seven. The next few years of my life are the hardest to remember.

The ministry provided individual and group counseling for people who struggled with homosexuality. I would do two sessions on the same day: one in the afternoon, one in the evening, with time for dinner between. I don't remember whether we met every week, every other week, or once a month, but all my hope for a better life began to revolve around those gatherings.

Once again, it was exhilarating to be able to tell people what I was going through without needing to explain anything. This brought joy for the first year or two.

I met a lot of nice, good-hearted people—committed Christians who wanted to do the right thing for themselves, their spouses, and their faith. My problem with pornography paled beside some of their stories of compulsive anonymous sex and broken marriage vows. I was surprised that most of these new friends lived in greater secrecy and shame about their identities. Some were pastors. Unlike me, they often felt too unsafe to confide in their church friends, wives, and husbands. They were leading double lives but craved integrity.

I didn't see things this way at the time, but everyone was marginalized and ineffective in their communities, vulnerable to emotional blackmail by the people they loved. Only in our support group did we find ourselves among equals, bound by a common curse.

After several years the program had a marked effect in my life. I felt closer to Jesus and had stopped buying pornography.

Ironically, the nights I drove alone to meetings in Toronto presented some of the worst temptations. Dining alone between sessions, I glimpsed nightlife in a big city for the first time. Once I drove to the corner of Church and Wellesley, the heart of Toronto's gay neighborhood, but I didn't stop or see anything unusual. Driving home in the dark, I would fantasize about truckers and sometimes pull off the highway to masturbate.

My marriage was troubled. I hardly remember what we argued about, but we often did. After four years, my wife revealed she had never loved me except for a few weeks while we were engaged. We started going to a marriage counselor, and she attended a support group for spouses of gay Christians.

About this time, an international ex-gay conference brought book authors and celebrities from the movement to speak in Toronto. I also had a chance to tell my story publicly. However, it was becoming obvious that Exodus could not promise true deliverance from homosexual feelings, only a plan for abstinence. Sure, gay Christians could lead a sexually pure life by being celibate or faithful in marriage, but never did I meet any gay man who credibly claimed to have lost his desire for other men.

But I had a strange shift in identity. I was not so ashamed of myself anymore. For the first time, I started to see homosexuality as a gift

God had given me, a special cross to bear, drawing me closer to Him. How else could I be at peace with myself? The ex-gay movement had given me several close friendships offering a new level of comfort and emotional affection. The Bible clearly valued this kind of love: for example, between David and Jonathan in the Old Testament. The New Testament even spoke of a "disciple whom Jesus loved," traditionally understood to mean the apostle John. I began to think of Jesus as my lover, and my faith entered a deeper mysticism.

My emotional pain deepened. The closer I felt to God, the more it removed me from belonging in the world. The Bible and Christianity reinforce the idea that we are only pilgrims passing through. To many the afterlife is more important than life, and this was becoming true to me. I had accepted that no human being could satisfy my intense desire for intimate connection, and nothing could deliver me from my sinful nature. The people in my support group might relate to this, but my wife and church friends couldn't understand my experience.

One Sunday afternoon the church held a meeting for all the men in our church. We talked about hopes and goals for our community. In the middle of this, I broke into tears. No one at the meeting spoke to me or asked what was wrong. It started to feel like I didn't belong in the church that had been another family to me for years.

Then came emotional paralysis. At night I started waking after three hours and couldn't get back to sleep. This lasted for months. Finally I couldn't face going to work. I liked gardening and going for walks. If it hadn't been for those activities and the company of my small daughters, I wouldn't have been able to get out of bed most days.

One day in the spring of 1995, I read a newspaper article about depression. This was the first time I recognized my feelings of listlessness and despair for what they really were. I was thirty-one.

Immediately I spoke to my doctor about mental health and was diagnosed with depression. Medication provided some relief but didn't help the fact that my closest relationships were coming apart. I also had clinical anxiety and panic disorder, but these went unrecognized by my doctor and would not be diagnosed until years later. Some antidepressants made me more agitated.

One day my doctor said, "Unless you accept your sexual orientation, you will not recover from depression."

Untreated depression is a terminal illness. I knew this from reading about the disease. I felt the impulse to end my suffering but didn't want to die.

"I can't accept my sexuality," I told my doctor. "My marriage will end. My church will ostracize me."

He guffawed. Several other members of my church were his patients. He knew and liked them, and he assured me they wouldn't react that way.

"You worry too much about what people think," he said.

It was a profound and simple truth about me. But what he didn't understand was how my church depended on people following the rules.

He sent me to see a social worker, a man whose first wife had come out as a lesbian. This man had a much different perspective from my own. I was terrified to meet him.

At our first appointment, I said, "Don't try to persuade me it's all right to be gay."

He didn't. He was respectful of my fears and only told me to be kind to myself.

He told me about his marriage, how he had loved his wife but needed to let her go. Their Unitarian congregation had supported both of them through the painful transition of divorce. They had moved on and found new life partners. His story seemed to reflect more the lovingkindness about Jesus I believed in than the censure and rejection I feared.

My church life continued to unravel. I'd been seeing my pastor regularly for counseling too: about my struggle with homosexuality, my depression, and my marriage troubles. He had been one of my best friends for many years, since long before I'd found help in the ex-gay movement.

One Sunday he delivered an angry sermon about Christians living too complacently. To lead people into relationships with God, we needed to break out of our comfort zones, he said. We needed to go into prisons and the places where people are downcast. This normally even-tempered man worked himself into a state of high excitement.

He shouted, "We have to learn to love the rapists, the pedophiles, and the homosexuals!"

I still didn't identify myself as gay, but it made me angry to hear gay people categorized this way. After the service I waited until almost everyone had left the church, then spoke to the pastor.

"How do you think someone who struggles with homosexuality would feel to be lumped together with violent criminals that way?" I asked.

I didn't ask him whether he was lumping me together with them.

He said there was no difference between these things. They were all sins, abominations in the eyes of God.

I argued, "You want people to feel welcome in this church. If there happened to be two lesbians sitting here today who have never tried to hurt anyone in their lives, they would be justified in finding you disrespectful."

We parted in tense disagreement. I went home, not realizing it would be my last Sunday at that church.

Meanwhile, I had bought some gay pornography, and my wife found it in my filing cabinet. I'd done this occasionally in the past and always acknowledged it to her in the end, but this time she was indignant. Refusing to have sex with me anymore, she asked me to sleep in the basement. The pastor called and offered to help, so we agreed to meet him.

At the meeting I said I didn't want to hurt our marriage, but for me to be healthy, I had to find a way to accept that I was gay. I had to start treating myself differently. I didn't know how to do this, I admitted.

The pastor said it was unacceptable for me to accept my feelings. This was unrepentance. He started to bellow, "Homosexuality is sin. God is disgusted with it. He is appalled. He hates it. He abhors it."

"Stop!" I said, getting up from my chair.

"Stop what?" He looked confused.

I left his office and paced around the waiting room. The door between the two rooms stood open. My wife and our pastor waited for me to calm down and return, but I wouldn't. They exchanged some glances and spoke quietly until she decided to leave.

Outside in the parking lot, she said, "That meeting must have been very difficult for you."

It was the first hint of empathy she had expressed to me in a long time. I was speechless.

Then she said, "It was hard for me too. After you left the room, he told me I have to love you."

A few days later, I called the pastor and said, "I can't talk to you anymore."

"Why not?"

"I'm trying to get well, and you're not helping."

When the summer break ended, I decided not to attend the ex-gay support group resuming in September. I'd even been invited to co-lead one of the support groups, but I refused. One of my best friends, the same counselor I had first spoken to when I'd phoned in desperation four years earlier, heard what was happening and phoned me. He had left New Directions over some doctrinal disagreement and was instead ministering to people at an AIDS hospice. I told him my whole grim story of the past few months.

He said, "I still believe homosexuality is a sin, but it's wrong for people to treat you that way. In fact, considering how depressed you are, it's harmful."

He conceded that I might need a break from New Directions, but the call brought little comfort. Even he didn't understand what I had begun to recognize: that in teaching me to deny and repress emotions, the ex-gay movement had contributed to my severe depression.

I had no one left who I could talk to safely except my doctor and the social worker. But alone at night, crying myself to sleep, I often felt Jesus sitting beside my pillow.

We believe whatever we need in order to survive. It's simple self-preservation. Religion shelters us from despair in the face of death. A profound, mystical relationship with Jesus Christ kept me alive through months of emotional trauma.

I drew comfort from my daughters, who turned two and four that fall. The older one helped me harvest potatoes, corn, and tomatoes from the big vegetable garden we'd planted together that spring. Being a father gave me another important reason to live.

One day my wife came home exultant from a visit to the doctor. She had tested negative for HIV.

"Don't you want to get tested?" she asked.

"Why should I?"

The leader of her spouse's support group at New Directions had suggested I must be having sex with men.

"She says that if gay husbands deny it, they must be lying," my wife said.

Someone who didn't even know me had passed judgment. My wife had been sensible in taking the precaution of getting tested. But revealing it this way after the fact, she had tried to catch me off guard and prove me untrustworthy.

"I don't need to get tested," I said. "I've lived in terror about that time with the guy in the car eleven years ago, and we didn't even do anything risky. I don't want to have an affair. I just want to find a way to celebrate who I am instead of hating myself."

But she was already convinced.

In hope of appeasing her, I started attending a twelve-step group for sex addicts to curb my compulsive appetite for pornography. It was a relief to participate in a support group again, and they didn't treat gay and straight people any differently. I asked someone to sponsor me, and we met for coffee.

After I told him my story, he said, "You're being too hard on yourself."

I didn't understand. I had a lifelong problem and was trying to fix it. Shouldn't it be hard?

In January, looking through some papers by our telephone, I un-covered a brochure for a divorce lawyer. When I confronted my wife, she said she wanted a separation. She had been planning to leave me. I was both devastated and relieved. I still loved her.

"I've been in rough shape lately," I admitted. "It has become very painful living here. I could use some time to myself. Maybe some time apart would be good for both of us."

I offered to move out, and she agreed. A few days later I was living in an apartment.

My doctor said, "Don't get into another relationship too quickly. Gay men coming out later in life need to figure out who they really are. Experiment a little."

I was flabbergasted. It seemed nobody understood me.

He asked how things were going with my friends in the church.

"Not very well," I said. "One of my best friends, who is also a patient of yours, came to see me. He wanted to hear the whole story from my mouth. When I finished, he was furious. He told me it was an abomination, then got up and left."

I don't know how the church handled my departure officially. By then they had gone through a process to establish charitable status, so taking discriminatory action as they had in the past might have led to more serious consequences. But I still experienced ostracism. Church people I met on the street turned and walked away or pretended not to see me. Others from my church might have acted more kindly or tried to listen, but by then I was too traumatized to handle more rejection. I stopped contacting people from the church, and they left me mostly alone. Over the next few months, I would receive a few letters from former friends telling me I was a bad person, justifying their own rude behavior.

For a long time afterward, I was terrified of all religious people. Over the years, I've become comfortable in their company again, even evangelical Christians. Occasionally I've encountered members of my old church. Some have treated me graciously and others have not, but

I don't need to take it so seriously now. I don't fear or seek approval from anyone who can't accept the kind of person I am.

Church services of any kind, I can't attend. The situation still reignites old trauma.

My understanding of the universe has changed completely. At first I stopped calling myself a Christian because I couldn't accept the hateful things people had done in Christ's name. My relationship with Jesus continued for a while. Faith in a higher power kept me alive until I learned to find strength in myself and the goodness of the world. My old church worshiped a god in the image of human narcissism, demanding utter allegiance and casting shame on every transgression. That belief system stopped making sense to me.

All people are imperfect, according to my old religion. That may be true, but I find it more useful to focus on what is good and remarkable about everyone. With more confidence in myself, I can respect the differences in others and enjoy their company. I'm seldom lonely now, but it has taken many years to learn to accept relationships for what they are, and to trust my own abilities. I don't worry so much about what people think.

But in the first few days after my church life ended, I found myself completely alone, starting a new social life. I had no idea what would happen next.

My sponsor at the twelve-step group for sex addicts introduced me to a gay Catholic priest. This man of God, who had himself relied for years on the support group, told me, "You're not a sex addict."

"Why do you say that?" I asked.

"You told me yourself you've been celibate since your wife kicked you out of the bedroom five months ago. Sex addicts don't have that kind of self-control. They're addicted to sex."

"What about masturbation and pornography? My life feels out of control to me."

The priest shook his head. "Don't worry about that. You're gay, and pornography is the only way you've found to express yourself. There's nothing wrong with having sex with men. When you have a normal, healthy sex life, these minor compulsive habits will stop feeling so powerful."

"Do you mean I can have sex with men and still have a relationship with God?" I asked.

"Yes."

At the time, it was what I needed.

That evening I sat alone at my apartment window. January 20, 1996. On the sidewalk below, snow fell out of darkness and sifted under streetlights.

I realized the separation with my wife would not be temporary. I was still in love with her, but she didn't want me. It had been a mistake, not just between two people, but the mistake of a whole community in trying to rub out something it didn't understand. I could never go back to that life.

I cried and prayed. I had been terrified of gay culture, had spent my whole life sheltering myself against it. Now I knew there must be good people and love in the world. I had to believe it. Hope was the only alternative.

Tomorrow I'd start over. I would have sex with a man. This time there would be no fear. It would be a choice. I would welcome the pleasure.

Narcissyphus

Samuel Peterson

I COULDN'T WAIT TO SCARPER UPSTAIRS WITH THE THIRTY-SIX-INCH inflatable Santa my grandma had sent me. I immediately sussed its potential. I had plans.

Upstairs in my bedroom, with the door closed as a tacit "do not disturb," I blew the pointy-headed vinyl out. I undressed quickly and then wrapped both myself and Santa in sheets. I was a centurion, a high-ranking officer in the Roman army. I had stumbled into a cave where I discovered a beautiful barbarian woman clad in furs. Our chemistry was undeniable. I swept her up into my muscular arms in a fiery embrace—I was reading a lot of sexy Greek mythology at eleven—and went in for the kiss.

I caught myself. In one of those stunning moments of pubescent mortification, I saw myself in the mirror: chubby, covered in sloppy drapery, hunched over a plastic pointy-headed Santa in a sheet toga. The entire tableau was horrifying. But past the humiliation of our peculiar romance, I had a revelation. I was a girl. I was a girl, and I had just sucked vinyl with a barbarian *woman*.

For years I framed this as a lesbian coming-out tale. Campy, silly, embarrassing preteen lesbianism. It would take decades to unpack this for what it actually was. I had been a Roman soldier, I had been a man: it was a story of an eleven-year-old transgender boy.

A couple years ago, I wrote a one-person memoir, a play called *F to M to Octopus*. It was a journal of transition with testosterone. In the play the character of myself says, "When I first saw my brother's tiny Vienna sausage, I immediately intuited: this (holding thumb and forefinger an inch apart) is why he gets treated differently." Because I understood gender difference then in terms of phallus/no phallus, I also intuited that there would be no magic solution for me, that I was what I was and I may as well surrender to that heartbreak. Never was I to kiss my elbow. Never would I ask God to make me a boy.

Within my family my tomboy nature was celebrated; it made me special to climb trees and be first chosen for kickball. I also saw masculinity in terms of privilege and interest. On our playground, in 1970s Northern Virginia, most boys were focused on blowing things up or trying to get the girls to pull down their panties. They were terrifying and revolting creatures mostly, except for my best friend David, with whom I played radio announcer, recording our broadcasts into our cassette tape deck for hours. And as the boys obsessed over girls' nethers, so did I obsess about theirs.

Over the years I became a secret curator of the male form. I had the greediest eyeballs, groping the stuffed-animal crotches of boys and men, carefully recreating the topography of muscle, developing my own personal taxonomy of pec varieties: the puffy, the hangdog, Michelangelo's David, the wolf. My forays into the sexual were always thrumming with subtext: did I *want* him or did I want to *be* him? And was my resentment of the unequal power dynamic the production of feminism, a movement I embraced with my soul, or because I was not free to be who I actually was?

As I got older, a sexual rapacity took me. While I identified as lesbian, dyke, I devoured men. I picked them up and fucked them like I was a predator. I often imagined there might be an element of cannibalism, that I was consuming their masculinity and power. In addition to power, I also sought annihilation. I was molested and raped by men. As a child I'd had no recourse, no part in this, but as an adult and burgeoning drug addict, and a secret trans man, I wanted immolation. In my self-loathing I placed myself in positions of inevitable violent harm.

This is not to say I am responsible for being raped. This is only a tiny insight into the mind that desires eradication of the body.

The reasons a young woman—even a repressed transgender man or woman—might be so hell-bent on erasure are complicated. I had always suffered from an unrelenting depression, I had become addicted to drugs and alcohol, and I found being seen and treated as something less than male enraging. Now that I have been out as a transgender man for some years, I can postmortem my actions as those of a deeply traumatized, insane woman. I can contextualize them as a refutation of my female body. I can say that I was destined to be a drug addict—what child steals money for chocolate and secrets away Honeycomb cereal boxes but an addict in training? My vexing gender only amplified the urgency to get wasted.

In 2007, at the age of forty-seven, I had been sober for some years. I fucked my last man as a woman in my first year of sobriety and dated only cis and trans women after that. I'd spent much of my adult life as a professional queer dyke, working for political lobbies, marching, making art. It never occurred to me that I might be anything other than a dyke. But in that year, the switch flipped.

My early sober years were peppered with newly transitioning people of all genders. Among my dyke friends, I would querulously query, "Haven't we made enough room to play with gender? Why would someone have to do that?" After all, I had capitulated to my gender, hadn't I? I framed my timid forays into masculinity as kink, a playful fetish of gendered roles. My girlfriend and I would pretend to be gay men in bed—it all just seemed very 2000, well within the dyke parameters of riot grrrls and strap ons. As for the trans women I dated, their stories seemed isolated, extreme, and perfectly understandable. I had no judgment beyond pure ignorance. My transphobia was largely reserved for female-to-male trans people.

Despite my queer dyke identity, I was still secretly eye-groping men. It was soothing to see their sweaty torsos, tight IT bands as they ran, the differences in geometry from feminine bodies. Although I would pluck my stray nip and chin hairs in what I can only articulate as near panic, I lost myself in the landscape of men's beard shadows, where the hair was sparse, where it met and flourished. My hairline was resolutely female; I pacified myself exploring the forehead maps of older men, canoeing their curves and peninsulas.

But it wasn't these secret glances that called out my masculinity. It was the woman I was dating. This particular woman identified as heterosexual. That wasn't necessarily a flag—I'd been in relationships with several women who'd ID'd as straight or bi. I never felt particularly rigid about my own sexuality, so why would I expect that in others?

What was different about this woman was that she was culturally straight. She had been groomed by familial design to behave differently with men. My family, by contrast, was a mixed bag of genders. I was raised by feminists. My mother was a highly successful analyst in the CIA, and my brother was a musical theater conductor. My male friends were never handy; they were intellectual, artistic. In no way did I actually connect being a man with fixing the sink or changing a tire or finding out if there was an intruder in the house. This woman treated me like she treated men, and it was an enormous turn-on. This woman and I were queering hetero gender roles—it was erotic and fun.

I began to experience a rather intrusive form of masculinity. I developed a phantom limb. Under the influence of severe heterosexuality, I began to experience a penis. It was maddening to crave a kind of penetration I could not initiate. The ghost penis haunted me.

I was at a twelve-step meeting. There was a person there, P, whom I suspected of being in FTM transition. I had observed the thickening face, the hair sprouting. We sat together, hugged, and quieted down for the recovery. Instead of the soggy saga of alcohol abuse and its comet-tail recovery, what I heard was a voice whispering in my right ear: "Ask P about testosterone." I shivered. "Ask P about testosterone." *Don't be weird*, I thought at the voice. "ASK P ABOUT TESTOSTERONE." *Okay, okay, Jesus! STOP IT!*

In the ensuing quiet, I did. I asked P about testosterone.

As life would have it, P wasn't transitioning with testosterone. P had just embraced P's butch realness. But the act of asking—a question that did not seem to originate with me and yet must have—burst open something in me like a time-lapse chrysanthemum. I was a forty-seven-year-old dyke, at least until that moment. Beyond that instant something began happening for me.

I suggested to my girlfriend that I might like to start injecting T. She accepted this information with mild bemusement; we were a fairly weird pairing, an outlier artist and a psychologist, so I imagine this intel wasn't entirely bizarre. We were accustomed to strange events, being an unusual couple, and when we were in love, we relished the strange nodes we seemed to branch. The relationship failed—not because I was transitioning but because it would have under any circumstance. I was inching toward fifty, a student in a technical college and a man wannabe.

Many trans people will tell you, regardless of their exterior presentation, "I am a real man," or "I am a real woman." I do not doubt the veracity and commitment of these statements. I can only say that for me, as an older trans guy, it was immensely frustrating, brutal even, to recognize my oblique failure at appearing male. My voice dropped, my clit raged into a massive thumb, and my body was altered. Yet I was still, for all my good efforts, mostly a changed chick. I recognized that the hormones would have their way with me, and that in good time, my neurochemistry and way of inhabiting my body would slip into a maleness, undefined by me and my desires and ideas, to be recognized by others.

It took a solid six years. A double mastectomy and hysterectomy shifted the shape tremendously. My inspirited practice of prayer and meditation, not to mention a heavy reliance on the shoulders of others, saved me from despair, and I was able to find meaning in my very public transition.

Now I am a man, or something akin to a man, or as much of a man as anyone is in any given moment, predicated on...what exactly?

I traveled from female to male, and I still can't tell you what precisely the difference is. Except that I am very, very different indeed.

I allow my greedy eyes license these days. They roam, still seeking the forms of men, finding comfort in the curl of hair above a collar, smelling the strong pitta from underarms and groins. I am a connoisseur of men's bodies still. In trans circles I'm often a youngster; despite being twenty to thirty years older than my trans brothers, I'm a baby T guy.

It's still awkward, learning to behave as a passable man. I hug like a woman. I'm effusive, ebullient. My vocal cadence isn't effeminate, it's feminine. Traces of an accent remain, masculinity as a second language. But I have learned that there are more ways to be a man than there are men.

I know my eyes will always roam. Someday these hands will too. These hands will outline a jutting collarbone with fingers, up a thick neck to trace a receding hairline. Someday these hands will caress the sweet sagging belly over muscle, twisting the hair as they make their way south. They will run fingernails up stubble and down a muscled back. They will cup the hard calves and run fingertips down the blade of the tibia; they will reach behind to catch the long sparse buttock hairs. Someday these eyes will get their fill of man, someday these hands will collapse on a chest and hold on, and I will fall into this beautiful, graceful man, and it will be me.

Crossing the Nueces

David Meischen

On Thursday, January 20, 1994, I drove from my home in Austin, Texas, to the Meischen family farm—a distance just short of two hundred miles. I was forty-five years old. I'd made this trip many times over the previous twenty-five years. The drive, carrying me south across the Nueces River and into the brush country of Jim Wells County—the drive was the least of it. I could not cross the Nueces without knowing that it divided two worlds. Call them before and after, family and others, farm and city, or small town and elsewhere. South of this personal border, David Meischen had always existed by means of a convenient and crippling lie. I'm sixty-six as I write this, and the lie still brushes up against me, still reaches out, still whispers, *Come home. Be one of us. Pretend. The cost is nothing. The cost is merely the truth of who you are.*

I'm a homosexual. *Girlie boy, sissy boy, queer bait, cocksucker, limp wrist*—there's something of me in most every insult I've heard about men who are attracted to men. And I was driving home to say so.

To my mother.

To my father.

The words I summoned that morning were the hardest words I've ever spoken and the most necessary. I saved my life by saying to my parents the words they'd invested a lifetime in training me not to say.

39

Elwood and Valerie Meischen never stood over me with a belt. Looking back now, I am stunned into awe, gratitude, sheer relief, remembering that my father never yanked me aside and said, *You will not play with Barbies when we're in town at your cousins'. You will not play hairdresser. You will not let your hands fly about you like butterflies.* Daddy never hit me for the sin of being myself, never called me names, though he didn't approve of my nancy boy ways. The occasional look told me so—unguarded moments when I caught him looking at me, the brief judgment I saw written there before he noticed that I'd noticed him looking and we both looked elsewhere. What I saw in my father's eyes was contempt, it was disgust, it was shame. What he didn't say, what I didn't put a name to even for myself, what happened between us when he saw that I saw him looking at me: these moments had more power than blunt words, our shared silences marking the divide between us.

These were moments only. They were not the whole of my life with my father. Daddy was a good man, dedicated to my mother, to the life they were building together, one difficult day at a time. In 1950, with drought threatening, he took a job at the bank in town. For all the years of my childhood—and many years beyond—he worked in town five days a week, half days on Saturday, *and* managed the grueling realities of life on a hundred acres of unirrigated brush country that only stubborn Germans would have thought to call a farm. My sister, my brothers, and I worked the fields with him. Judi, Larell, Vance, and I—we knew without question that our father loved us. The work told us so. His dedication to our mother told us so. But Daddy's love was not selfless, expressive, unconditional. It was moody, irascible, demanding, inflexible. His love bound us to him, and the terms were not negotiable. We did what we were told. Or else.

We planted, hoed, and harvested beside him, fed the animals by the strict schedule he demanded, butchered hogs and made sausage under his tutelage. The work, the hours we spent together—these bound us to him as surely as the unspoken love that informed them. How difficult, then, for one of us to say or do anything that ran counter to the life our father built for us. For me, even the idea of being gay, of *anyone* being gay, was simply not thinkable. I didn't have the words, even in private. In early adulthood, when I'd found the words, when I could imagine a world in which I lived as a gay man, I spun an ugly little fantasy in which I said to my father that I was gay—but only out of anger, using the words as a weapon to inflict pain. At my angriest, when I was desperate to break free of Daddy, I knew I wouldn't actually tell him I was gay. I might be able to envision that life, but it was a life I didn't want.

You see, my mother loved me too. Her mother loved me, her sisters too. And my father's mother. Sissy boy that I was, I was at home in the company of women. They didn't send me out of the room, didn't insist I go outside and do guy things with the guys, though there was a price to pay. In the fall of 1955, for example, during my first semester of first grade, I made a spectacle of myself at bat, so utterly inept that my teacher, a wonderfully kind widow in her midfifties, walked to the plate and helped me, cradling my arms in hers, holding my hands where they held the bat, helping me swing as the ball crossed the plate.

In third grade, I learned a harder public lesson. I don't remember when I discovered skipping rope, but by 1957 I quite liked it. I liked what skipping rope did to my pulse, my breath. I loved how fast my feet could move, all in one place as the rope spun the air around me into a single ecstatic note lasting as long as I could keep it going, hyper and happy and lost in the light filtering down through mesquite trees that dappled the playground. Years later, as an adult coming to terms with being gay, I latched onto the expression *light in the loafers*—a nearly perfect euphemism for men like me. Whatever insult might live inside the expression has long since leached away, leaving me with a memory of myself at nine skipping rope.

I skipped rope at recess. With the girls. And that's what the boys called me. *Girl.* A single word, single syllable, repeated like an echo. My peers were still short in the repertoire of insult. The word *queer* showed up a year or so later, and I only ever heard it tossed out in mock accusation, as if no one in Orange Grove, Texas, could possibly—*actually*—be queer, whatever that was. But when the boys called me *girl*, they meant it. Think what lesson the girls internalized, hearing something essential about themselves turned into an instrument of humiliation.

I remember that year as the most difficult of my first two decades. I remember a stretch of weeks when misery weighed so heavy in me, I would open a book, set the upright V of it on the desk in front of me, put my head down behind it, and wonder how I would manage to breathe through another moment, another hour, another day of school. Until a lucky morning when I looked at the wall calendar in my classroom and noticed the summer months were near. I identified the very last day of school and then counted the schooldays left. One by one I marked them off.

And didn't tell a soul. Putting my playground humiliation into words would have breached the barrier between school and home, would have given voice to the looks my father gave me when I behaved like someone who would rather skip rope than learn to handle a bat. I wanted simply to be done with school, to be home with my family. My father's looks notwithstanding, I felt safe with him and my mother, with my sister and brothers, with aunts, uncles, cousins, grandparents. I suppose I have denial to thank for the wonderful times I had in the company of kin. They looked right at me and didn't see what they were seeing—daydreaming David Meischen, who flitted through childhood and adolescence like a kite in need of tethering, who ached when he looked at men and didn't let himself know what that meant, who conflated the insult attached to his behavior with an essential inner something that spun him like a jump rope, yearning in a way that clearly other men did not, weaving fear and love into an ever-stronger force field between what he intuited about himself and what might be spoken in the presence of his mother and father.

Somewhere during these years—sixth grade? seventh?—my mother had a gentle conversation with me at a moment when no one else was around. We were sorting laundry, of all things, when she said that it was okay I didn't participate in sports, didn't belong to a team, didn't put down whatever I was reading and head outdoors when my brothers wanted a round of practice pitching. But—always a *but* in this kind of parent talk—why not take an *interest* in sports? I'd have something to talk about with the guys. I'd have more friends.

I remember numerous private conversations with my mother. These were never effusive or self-involved, never analytical, never addressed to the inner life. My mother loved me, but she rarely used words such as *love*. She was a matter-of-fact woman, focused on the practical necessities of how to get along in the only world she knew. It was Mother who told me, when I got old enough to wonder why my paternal grandmother lived by herself, that my father had lost his father to suicide. Mother gave me an explanation suitable for four-year-olds, followed by a rule that all of us learned by heart. *We don't talk about this in front of your father.* This is what we didn't do: we didn't bother our father with anything we thought might bother him. I didn't need to tell myself that same-sex attraction fell into the same category as my grandfather's self-inflicted end.

Two words characterize the divided life that was mine. Two words: *farm* and *family*. The Meischen homestead is a hundred acres of shallow soil cleared from the brush country along Agua Dulce Creek, a hundred miles south of San Antonio and fifty miles inland from Corpus Christi Bay. The Meischens took up residence here in 1929—my father, age five, his twin brothers, age six, and their parents. Daddy put down roots here, deep roots, and never left. I think that explains part of my attachment to this piece of land. My grandmother was widowed here; she and my father kept the place going when the war came. Daddy's brothers spent three years in the South Pacific. When they returned from the war, they found other pursuits. In 1946, when my mother became a Meischen, she moved onto the home place with her husband and his mother. I arrived in 1948, second child, first son. Until 1952, when my second and last brother was born and Grandma built a house in town, I lived among the sounds of German. My sister and I shared an especially close bond with Grandma; she was intimately involved in our crucial early years.

Meischen kinfolk were in and out of the house where I grew up. We alone lived on a farm, a magical place where relatives could visit and enjoy the fresh air, the freedom of the open acres, without the work the place demanded. One of my father's brothers settled in Orange Grove; we spent so much time with his family that his children were more like siblings than cousins. My mother was the oldest of five, all Catholic. My sister and I, eldest cousins on the Catholic side, spent much of our childhood and adolescence diapering and riding herd on our younger cousins. I loved this part of growing up, loved taking care of the little ones during family gatherings. I suppose I gravitated toward them, at least in part, because they looked up to me in the way younger children tend to admire older children—as opposed to male cousins nearer my age, who had little use for me and my sissy boy ways. As I see it, an essential part of me is that I was born to be a father, to be involved in the care and raising of children.

In a classic paradox, it was family that made me live the lie that I was straight, family that saved me from the damage of living the lie. Father and mother, sister and brothers, aunts, uncles, cousins, grandparents—they kept me in line. And loved me for walking the line. They nourished me with food and drink, with conversation and laughter and dancing—in the babble of their voices, the promise of becoming a father, a promise that endured. At twenty-eight I married. At thirty-one and thirty-three, I ushered my sons into the world. I loved my wife. I made a private pledge never to leave my marriage. I tried. It was an exhausting exchange—living the mind-over-matter life—a gradual erosion of will until a spring season in my early forties when I began to dismantle the wall I'd built around my knowledge that I am gay. A bleak year followed, as I surrendered to what felt inevitable. I said to my wife that I could not go on. I came out to my sister and brothers. And then, the damages accruing, I faced my sons and exposed the falsehood their father had been living.

Why not leave my parents out of it, as my sister and brothers advised? Daddy was sixty-nine years old, deeply enmeshed in a narrow and inflexible view of the world, his grown children subscribing to the mantra our mother, our family, our culture, our religious teaching had breathed into us from birth: *Do not upset your father.* This commandment had kept all of us in line. And I had my mother's health to consider. Approaching her sixty-sixth birthday on the day I drove to the farm to un-say the lie about myself, Mother was five and a half years into her struggle with ovarian cancer. Why not feed my parents bromides to explain my divorce? Why not let them live out their days explaining their eldest son to themselves as simply the family eccentric, the oddball uncle, curiously single after a seventeen-year marriage, living in crazy, liberal Austin?

Let me answer with a question. Why bother at all then? Why sever myself into halves—openly gay man for my days in Austin, closeted uncle for visits with my family in South Texas? The only way to make myself whole, to have any hope of an integrated life, was to step into the presence of the most important members of the family that shaped me, the family that would shape every future visit home, to say to them the truth we'd invested so many years, so much energy, in not seeing. *Plain as the nose on your face*, as Mother was fond of saying. *Been a snake, it would have bit you.*

If my mother is to be believed, what I said that day was as unsettling as a rattlesnake curled beside the back steps. Not that I walked in and sprang the truth on them. I sat down on the couch in the living room. Daddy settled into his recliner opposite me. Mother sat beside him, closer to me, in her rocking chair. I don't remember a single detail from the knotted skein of words I unraveled on my way to the word *gay*. I started by saying that my marriage was coming to an end, that the reason had to do with me. I faltered, tried again, faltered. How do you say the one thing your life has trained you not to say, with courage in hiding and habit so deeply rutted you despair at climbing out of it? Tears came at some point. I was aware without being aware that my parents remained receptive. They didn't lean forward, didn't encourage me. But there was no sign of the hostility that reared up in Daddy when he sensed he was about to be crossed. Did he let me say what he didn't want to hear because he could see how badly I needed to? I don't know. I do know that, finally, I managed to say, "I'm gay."

My mother rose from her chair. She lay claim to the word *flabbergasted*. She stepped across to me. "Of all the things you might have come here to say, never in my wildest dreams…" She delivered these words with the bluntness Valerie Meischen was known for when she was out of patience. And then, the clincher. My mother put her hand on my shoulder, and her voice changed. "But you're our David." And I was whole. Not forever. Not with the instantaneous alchemy that makes personal transfiguration so appealing in the pages of myth. But—for a single, breathtaking moment—whole to the woman who had given birth to me.

I had lunch with my parents. As I departed for Austin, I turned and tried to say something reassuring. Daddy waved me on, his voice ragged with pain. This was his first reaction. As he said in a letter he wrote six days later, "The reason we didn't say much is because we were speechless and holding on to each other." And then he let me have it. He challenged my decision to break up the only family my sons knew. The bulk of his letter, he devoted to my mother's prolonged struggle against cancer, saying it had been thoughtless and selfish of me to add to her burden. He referenced the fact that I am gay only in closing: "There will be no discussion of your new so-called lifestyle, and don't ever try to bring one of your significant others to our home." (Yes, he actually said *lifestyle* and *significant others*. I still have the letter. My theory is that Daddy picked up these terms listening to Rush Limbaugh and others who mocked all things new in the world.)

I've spent years considering the point Daddy raised about my sons. I still don't have an answer, except to admit that I had no right to upend the only life they knew. I know the prevailing platitude. What good would I have been to Karl and Jack as an unhappy father trapped in an unhappy marriage? I might answer that many an unhappy man has stayed in an unhappy marriage and raised children with reasonable success. I want to say that I couldn't make myself. But the truth is I *chose* to end my marriage. My sons survived. They have turned into wonderful young men. But I can't say I did them any favor by divorcing their mother. As a friend said to me when I was agonizing over this decision, there is no control group for divorce, no separate scenario in which a hypothetical version of me would stay married so that I might study the difference. No. I sundered my marriage. Credit, blame, responsibility—all three belong with me.

As for what my father said about my mother. Yes, the news was an added burden at a difficult time. But it wasn't thoughtless; it was the result of painful, insistent thinking. I have never regretted letting my mother know who I am. She died knowing me, having known me. My sister and one of my brothers were furious with me for coming out to my parents. Both my brothers were married (still are) and fathers. My sister remarried several years later (her first husband died of cancer). All three went to the altar in public ceremonies. All three wear wedding bands. All three display photos of themselves coupled. No one has asked them to hide this essential part of themselves.

My mother died on May 13, 1995. She died on the family farm, with her husband and her four children at her side. Her last breath slipped away a few hours before Mother's Day, a year and four months after hearing that her firstborn son is gay. Two weeks before her death, on Friday, April 28, I drove to the farm for a visit. My divorce had gone through in December. This much Mother knew. She didn't know that my ex-wife was planning to remarry, that my younger son would move to Anderson Island, Washington, to live with her and her new husband, that my older son would move into a new house in Austin with me. The doctors taking care of Mother had run out of options. Knowing that her days were numbered, I had decided not to tell her about events that would put two thousand miles between my sons. But somehow on Saturday morning of our last visit, I slipped up in front of her and said something about the new house. When she asked for details, I briefly summed up what was coming and told her that if she wanted to know more, I would be glad to talk with her at length. Mother said she'd like that. Then she leaned toward me in a mother-son gesture I knew all too well and said, "Let's wait until your father drives to town this afternoon."

When the house was empty except for us, we sat in the living room and talked. Mother went straight to what was uppermost in her mind—the day I'd said I am gay. She had committed the date to memory. More than a year had passed, she said, and she hadn't told her sisters. It bothered her, Mother said, that Aunt Lee and Aunt Isabel had confided in her at difficult moments and she had not confided in them about me. She felt almost as if she'd betrayed an understanding between them. I said, "Mother, please, if you want to tell Aunt Lee and Aunt Isabel I'm gay, say it. You have my permission." Her worry was that if her sisters knew, they might say something to their husbands. What if word got out? What if one of our kin said something insulting? Then Mother paused and said, "Well, I guess you've heard those words before." I assured her I was thick-skinned enough to withstand a bit of mockery from an uncle or a cousin.

This was to be our last sit-down conversation. I've never forgotten that we spoke without disguises, that she spoke to me as a known person, spoke about how she had come to know me more completely, spoke without fear or recrimination knowing I am gay. *My mother knew me.* Who among us would not want that?

That weekend has a coda. I left the farm Sunday, April 30, and returned to Austin. The following Tuesday evening, the phone rang. It was Mother. She sounded tentative and apologetic and far away. She said she'd thought about it and decided not to say anything to her sisters. We spoke briefly about other things and hung up.

Here's what happened. I have no eyewitness testimony, but I know it in my bones. Mother told Daddy what she and I had talked about. Before she could finish saying she might tell her sisters that her son is a homosexual, Daddy said no. I knew my father, his moods, his insistence that the world he knew was entitled to his opinion on all things that matter, his insistence that my *lifestyle*, my *significant others*, if any, were not to be mentioned. Then he stood there while she called me, making sure the lie of not telling had slammed the door on us again.

Daddy was just short of seventy-one when Mother died; he had the vitality of a much younger man, paired with a view of the world that did not brook change or challenge. Two years later, I met and fell in love with Scott Wiggerman. Often during the coming years, I made a joke about my father's capacity for denial: had I phoned him to announce that I was straight after all, that I'd met the perfect woman, that Scott and I were done, it would have taken my father a day and a half to forget I'd ever spoken the word *gay* in his presence.

I no longer remember when or how Daddy was informed of Scott's arrival in my life. And I suppose now is the time to confess that if sins of omission count—and I'm convinced they do—I've had countless brief visits to the closet in the years since I decided to live openly gay. I could have told my father about Scott in the same way—and with the same sense of urgency—as I told my sister. I've been open with Judi since I came out to her, which is to say I know that she knows and accepts Scott's place in my life. I never feel myself editing our relationship in her presence—by not mentioning Scott, by mentioning him as if we are merely friends. But I delayed telling my father, even as Scott and I made explicit vows to a committed, exclusive relationship, even as we planned a life together, bought a house together. In the presence of straight men who look or sound like the men I grew up knowing, I reach the moment where Scott—his name, our relationship—would flow into the conversation. And suddenly I'm tongue-tied. I can see it coming, and I fumble anyway—honesty coming up against caution, the dissembler in me assuming the next moments will turn out just right if certain words are not spoken.

Perhaps, in a way, my father did me a favor by refusing to acknowledge my relationship with Scott. He reminded me—about being gay and loving Scott—that while these are as natural to me as breathing, they are also as important. That to keep breath in me, I must face my life as a continuous coming out, as a daily acknowledgment of myself and the man I spend my life with.

With Daddy it was never easy. The first real test came shortly after Scott and I moved in together, when my father announced that he was planning to marry again. He drove his fiancée to Forth Worth to meet one of my aunts, a drive that took him within two hundred yards of our house. He didn't stop to say hello. On the return drive, he met another of my aunts at an Austin restaurant, and I played the weasel, leaving Scott at home for a few minutes of shamefully dishonest banter. I cringe remembering, partly because it was *so easy* to do the wrong thing.

With my father's wedding approaching, I summoned the courage to ask that Scott be included. Daddy's no was as blunt as it had always been; he left no room to maneuver, no room to broach the subject again. That's what I told myself then. But I was forty-eight years old when my father refused to invite Scott to his wedding. I had lived on my own, supporting myself, since I was twenty. I had married and raised two sons. I had thrived among the challenges of public school teaching for more than two decades. I had found the courage to face up to being gay. I could have called my father a second time, a third, a fifteenth. I could have driven to the farm and appealed to him in person. I could have written a long letter spelling out my case. I did none of these.

Later, when I found the nerve to face up to my father, I fell back on surly, pouting hardheadedness. Once during a head-butting session, he accused me of being stubborn. I almost laughed out loud. I paused and said, "Daddy, tell me I came by that honestly." The implication stopped him cold. I didn't change his mind about anything, but he clearly knew that I knew where I had learned to be harshly, insistently self-righteous.

For the remaining years of his life, this man refused to have Scott on the farm, rebuffed any chance to set foot in our house, though he didn't reject Scott's company entirely. Early on, as a compromise of sorts, my father agreed to Scott's presence at restaurants and other neutral locations. At first, I was grateful, but after several years of these gatherings, painstakingly arranged by my sister, each felt more absurd than the last—Daddy and his new wife at one end of a restaurant table, often with one of my sons beside them, others in the middle of the table, and Scott at the far end with my sister, the family peacemaker. Eventually, Scott opted out, and who could blame him? Why spend time in the presence of a man you don't even know, a man who clearly would rather you didn't exist, a man who has done his best to drive a wedge between the man you love and the family he was born into?

Had my mother been with us, I don't think Daddy would have gone to his grave saying no. She'd have given him a year to let his good heart come to the fore. Then one day she'd have aimed a piercing gaze at him across the top of her glasses and said, "Elwood, honestly, enough already. Get yourself ready. We're going to Austin." I've only ever known two people who could maneuver my father out of a corner he wouldn't let himself get out of. One was his mother, the other mine—neither available for the task at hand. Besides, this messy struggle wasn't theirs. It was mine.

About my sister and brothers, whom I love dearly, let me say that they were only doing what we'd always done—trying to please our father, letting him have his way—while I continued to break the rules. My sister's role was simply untenable. Judi works harder at the daunting challenges of family coexistence than anyone I know. She did what she could to please a father who often refused to be pleased. She reached out to both of us—her gay brother, who expected Scott to be embraced by the family, and her father, who adamantly refused. The task she accepted was like negotiating compromise between brothers on opposite sides during the American Civil War, brothers estranged by a shared language.

Often during the early years with Scott, I simply wanted to be done with the Meischens of South Texas—for two reasons. One was the appeal of a clean break: how much simpler to deal with a difficult family by not dealing with them at all. The other was petty: allowing myself to play the self-righteous role in one of those ludicrous scenes from soap operas—or sleazy daytime talk shows—delivering justice by way of an overblown rant. I would climb to the high ground, feeding on vengeance.

Lucky for all of us, I had access to a reliable therapist. More than once when I felt flummoxed by the situation with my father, I went for a series of sit-downs. My therapist was an expert in the art of the necessary question, the hard question, the question that instigates change. Halfway through a session where I expected a stamp of approval for the feelings roiling in me, he stopped me with a question that answered itself. "You do realize—don't you—that your intolerance of your father's intolerance is intolerance?"

I remember thinking, *This is going to cost me.* It did. Aside from the checks I wrote for more sessions, I had years of hard work ahead. But I wanted a relationship with my father. If I could lay aside resentment, I could open myself to the love I felt for the man who'd fathered me. I could accept that he loved me only so far as he was able, that none of us loves perfectly. One of the hardest lessons of my life, then, has been that I cannot—*should* not—make another person do the right thing, whatever that is, cannot shape another person to my own ends no matter the motive. Harder still: getting up each morning and facing myself in the mirror, facing who I am, planting a flag for that person.

There were days, still, even late in my father's life, when I wanted a clean break, but I knew the damage it would do, the ugly moral indignation. Breaking away from my father, from the family I was born into, would have created another version of the divided self: half a life denying my gay identity, half a life denying those who'd formed me. As I have often said to Scott, every good thing in me I can trace to my father—his work ethic, his loyalty to those he loved, his persistence in the face of hardship, his sense of humor. Every flaw too—mood swings, anger, self-righteousness, a pattern of judging others, a deep-seated conviction that the world owes me something. My father lives in me with every breath I take.

In the late summer of 2013, I called Daddy to let him know that Scott and I would get married that October in Taos, New Mexico. I had no intention of inviting my father to the wedding and no expectation that he would express so much as a neutral opinion. Scott suggested I save myself the bother and let Daddy know about our wedding after the fact. Or let him find out by way of the family grapevine. My sons said much the same. Why let their grandfather break the continuous chorus of congratulations that rained on us from everyone who heard about our upcoming wedding? But I'd spent too many years not telling my father what he didn't want to hear—and feeling with each little act of cowardice that I was making short work of shame, letting it germinate from within.

On the afternoon we spoke, Daddy was several weeks short of his eighty-ninth birthday. Age had gentled him, had made him frail. But my news got his dander up; it put a bit of the old truculence back in his voice. He pronounced our wedding plans foolish and then tumbled into a rant that sounded like an aged Rush Limbaugh free-associating. I almost laughed when he happened upon abortion. Not that the subject itself is funny—but that, gay wedding or not, Scott and I were not likely ever to consider terminating a pregnancy. My part in the conversation was to say, "Daddy, I'm not going to argue abortion with you." After which he asked me a string of those ludicrous yes/no questions to which any sane answer is something else entirely. Each time I responded that I hadn't called to argue. Eventually, he ran out of steam, and the conversation was over.

That call was to be the last act in the process of my coming out to my parents. By year's end, Daddy's health had begun to fail. In March of 2014, after months of back pain, doctors identified a malignant tumor on his lower spine. Surgery was out of the question, but radiation treatments shrank the tumor and left him without pain. He spent about three months at home on the farm with our stepmother and, when that proved untenable, moved himself into a nursing center in George West, some two dozen miles north. I drove down while Daddy was having radiation treatments, drove down to help out when he went in to have his pacemaker battery replaced, drove down simply to spend time with him on the farm and at the nursing center. The point now was to breathe the same air as my father, to be there with him, to let him know that I loved him, to do for him the little things he could no longer do, as he had done for me during my infancy and childhood, as he would have done for any of his adult children had we needed him.

Need is the important word here. During the year of his failing health, I didn't need my father's stamp of approval, didn't need a deathbed change of heart. Need was on his side now. Daddy needed my sister and brothers; he needed me. Our needs were simpler—and easily satisfied. We needed his company, needed whatever time was left of his presence in our lives, nothing more.

After the pacemaker procedure, I drove Daddy and my stepmother back to the farm, a distance just short of fifty miles. Leaving the hospital, as I turned onto Ocean Drive, the hatchback door lifted open; I hadn't shut it properly. My father decreed that I would stop right there and shut it—not advisable in the traffic on Ocean Drive. By the time I turned into a side street, pulled over, and stopped, Elwood Meischen was out of patience as only Elwood Meischen could be. Minutes later, his voice filled with disgust when it became apparent I didn't know Corpus Christi's freeway system like the back of my hand. In the midst of his running commentary on this shortcoming, he several times pronounced that I was driving too fast, that only one of my siblings drove at a sane speed. It doesn't matter which; his aim was to show me that I'd been measured and found wanting. We'd only gone fifteen miles when it was time to stop for burgers. I didn't do that right either. Fifteen miles and he'd reminded me of every single thing about him that had pissed me off in the six-plus decades I had known him.

He was my father. I loved him anyway.

In February of 2015, Scott and I drove to Albuquerque and picked out our new house. When we returned to Austin, my father had been through a medical ordeal that sounded like something out of Kafka, with two sixty-mile ambulance rides, a nursing staff on one end that seemed to have their hands tied, a urologist on the other who didn't want to bother seeing a patient at the emergency room, a urinary tract infection that was entirely avoidable. On March 3, Judi called to say she thought our father was near the end. I drove down that afternoon. Daddy knew me when I entered the room. I was certain at least that he knew my voice. But he seemed to exist in two places at once—in the room with us (my brothers were there when I arrived) and wherever his visions were taking him. Even when he said nothing, it was clear another sphere overlapped the one we could see. Daddy's eyes moved about the room, not a random search pattern fueled by fidgets but the movement of eyes focusing in turn on a series of visitors visible only to him.

We decided not to leave him alone at night. My youngest brother stayed with him Tuesday night. I drove to Corpus Christi and spent the night with my sister and brother-in-law. Wednesday morning I drove back to George West. I spent the day with Daddy and then took up night vigil in the room with him. I fell asleep and woke, fell asleep and woke again, each time roused by a frightened cry from my father's bed. He was beyond coherence, mostly even beyond words, but each time he cried out, I took his hand and told him I was there, assured him he was safe, assured him he was loved. Each time he quieted. It was my voice, I'm sure, that soothed him—a familiar voice even if he no longer had a name for it. But I did. David. Elwood's son.

Thursday morning my sister arrived, and by early afternoon, I was on my way back to Austin. Saturday morning, before I could make plans to drive down again, my brothers called to say that Daddy was gone. They had been in the room with him; they had been talking to each other while he slept. Our father breathed his last so quietly, Larell and Vance didn't notice until they heard how quiet the room had become.

I wrote and delivered Daddy's eulogy. My sons were there, my daughter-in-law; my siblings and their families; aunts, uncles, cousins; family friends and neighbors by the dozen. But not Scott. He'd been a stranger to my father. And my father to him. Because Daddy hadn't wanted to know him, Scott felt like a stranger in the family that had shaped me. He couldn't imagine attending a stranger's funeral among strangers.

So be it.

I returned from the funeral, said goodbye to my sons and daughter-in-law, and plunged into the final stages of packing. On March 23, I spent fourteen hours on the road with our somewhat freaked-out cat. Here in Albuquerque, I supervised roof repairs, new flooring, a twelve-foot-by-twelve-foot built-in bookcase with library ladder. Scott stayed behind and closed up the house in Austin. On April 19, he flew home to me.

Here, on the northwestern edge of Albuquerque—canyons carved of volcanic rock, tumbleweed windstorms, desert landscape, desert air, desert sky—here, my father's death seems as insubstantial as a shimmer of sun on the distant horizon. Here, I walk for miles with Scott, a new life unfolding before us. Here, the Rio Grande separates not one country from another but two parts of our city. Here, folks pronounce the *e* in *Grande*. Here, the Nueces River recedes to the memory of a line that no longer divides—on the other side, a world no longer mine. The tie was my father. I claim him, if not the ties that bound him to the lie that once bound me.

Caged

Anil Kamal

As I sit at my desk staring out the window, I notice streaks of dirt and bird poo. My cubicle is a square desk, drab and boring as hell. The fabric partition is a steel grey with the overhead cabinets a light taupe. Not one photo or personal item adorns my sterile environment. I could be describing a prison cell, which is apt because I feel like a confined inmate.

My body is still. I'm just sitting here, a patient public service employee, waiting for the phone to ring, an email to pop up, or a colleague to pass by. Anything to make me forget the ball of heat that's bouncing against my chest cavity.

The windowpanes on the building across the street reflect the flags on top of my building. They billow and flourish in the crisp April wind. Just below the flags, I can make out the faint reflection of my face. Unlike those flags that fly for peace and freedom, I am motionless. I look very unhappy, like a caged bird sitting in front of a bolted door, yearning to spread its wings.

Here come the shivers. My body is preparing for the trauma that my mind is about to inflict in the form of my worst fear being exposed. Every lie that I've told myself, every forbidden emotion that I've swallowed, all of it is boiling over, but the heat being generated isn't enough to warm me up. Each jolt that shakes my flesh and scatters goose bumps across my skin is *the secret* proclaiming itself in advance of my revelation.

The time has come.

The office is dead quiet. Most people won't start trickling in for another fifteen minutes. I have some final moments of solitude with my deep dark secret. It's no longer resting at the back of my mind but is be-bopping against the walls of my head, trying to compete with my thumping heartbeat.

Another wave of shivers rolls across my skin. I am being shaken into realization.

"Hi, Pony!"

Thank God. A voice to break me away from myself. I spin my chair around and see Danielle beaming at me, her arms outstretched for a mandatory hug. She and I are cubicle buddies. This is the first time that I'm laying eyes on her in about four months. She took some personal leave to sort herself out from a bunch of personal drama. Danielle had it right. Know your limits, realize when your mind needs a break, and take the appropriate amount of time to heal away from the exhaustion of everyday life. I wish I could have done the same, but that would have meant me having to call in sick indefinitely.

My angst is washed away by sudden joy as I jump out of my chair and rush into Danielle's outstretched arms. I don't want to let her go. Because if I do, I'll have to look into her eyes and then she'll know. Shit, the tears are starting to brim, and pretty soon I'll dissolve into a snotty mess. I can't do this here.

Danielle pulls away from me and scans my face like it's a barcode, trying to compute each furrow on my pre-crying face. I should really be comforting her, asking her how she's been and how everything is at home, but it's quite evident that I need her full attention.

"Pony, what's wrong?"

Pony is Danielle's pet name for me. We were gabbing about our childhood love for *My Little Pony* one day as she teased me for prancing around, and it stuck. Danielle is a few years older than I am—thirty-six to my thirty-two. She is so much more than a work colleague. She's a big sister and confidante, and being her friend feels like home.

Well, this is it. I need to tell her, and I need to tell her right now. Thirty-two years have whittled down to one sad little Tuesday morning at the office, right before our ritualistic cups of coffee. Confession before caffeine. The adrenaline should be more than enough to keep my eyes open.

I grab hold of Danielle's hands (they're so warm compared to my icy claws) and stare into her emerald eyes.

"I have to tell you something, right now."

The shivering has returned with intensity. There is no way I can hold this in until lunch, and there isn't any time to leave the building. My mind is about to vomit, and there's no stopping the retch that's about to spew forth. Not an attractive image, I know, but that's what it feels like. Danielle furrows her brows together and clasps my hands inside her heated grip.

"Okay, let's go."

She leads me through the maze of cubicles as if I were a child being guided by his mother across a busy street. The elevator ride down to the basement is a quiet one, which is abnormal for the two of us, as we're usually chirping at each other. Away from the eyes of office busybodies, we enter the abandoned food court, long closed for business because of expensive leases. It is my turn to lead, and I pull Danielle toward the farthest corner. All the tables are those mideighties Formica ensembles with built-in plastic seats that have little indentations for your butt. One size does not fit all, especially if you've been carb overloading while sitting on your ass for eight hours on the daily.

You never choose where a life-changing moment will happen, do you? If it were up to me, we'd be lounging on a plush purple chaise sipping from crystal champagne flutes, but alas, we are not the Real Housewives of Ottawa. We squeeze ourselves into a two-seater table and sit across from each other.

Adding to the hideous décor are floor-to-ceiling mirrors that line the walls. I despise mirrors as much as any bloodthirsty vampire. I wish I was one so I wouldn't have to ever see myself. At the age of thirty-two, I am unable to look at my reflection head-on for more than two seconds without the rush of shame flooding through my body. To look any longer would expose the delicate charade that I've been putting on since puberty. It's time to confront my fears, not only in front of Danielle but also myself.

The performance is over.

I can't stomach looking anywhere but at the two sets of hands clasping each other on the scuffed linoleum table. White pale hands intertwined with brown ashy ones. Even my skin is making a statement. Danielle's face is taut, her eyes wide saucer plates heaped with worry.

"Okay, what is it?" she asks.

"You already know."

"I do?"

"Yes. You tell me."

"Pony, you're scaring me. What is it? Are you sick? Is it cancer?"

What? Cancer? Oh God, she thinks I'm dying. Maybe a part of me is going to die. These are the last rites for Anil's Worst Kept Secret.

"No. I'm not sick. You know, Danielle. You tell me."

Danielle sucks in a column of air and tightens her grip on my hands. She has always known, and like a true friend, she tells me what I don't have the courage to say out loud to her, to myself, and to our reflections standing vigil like two deathbed nuns in the mirrors.

"Okay, what, are you gay?"

Gay. Fuck, she said it. It's out there. It's done. Everything that I've tried so hard to repress my entire life has now been exposed by the one word I feared being called.

"Yes."

Yes. I did it. I couldn't say the actual word myself, but I admitted it. Close enough, right?

That one-word declaration has left me empty as I have nothing left to hide. I lean over the table, place my head over our clasped hands, and weep. I have thirty-two years' worth of crying to do, so it takes a few minutes to exhaust my tear ducts.

As I slobber over our hands, Danielle sits patiently, radiating a tenderness that wraps around my body like a security blanket. I bawl for a few more seconds, then draw my head up and blink my eyes to focus through the tears at the first person in my circle that I've come out to. What is she thinking, and what the hell will she say? Everything is going to change, but will it affect our friendship? How could it not?

"Okay, and?"

And? What does she mean *and?* That's it, baby. My whole life is now an open book—a children's book with enormous pop-up pictures and a little cartoon cutout guy holding an *I'm here. I'm queer. Get used to it!* sign fluttering about.

"And? There is no and!"

"I thought you were sick! I thought you were dying or something!"

Well, something did die, didn't it?

"Are you okay with it? Do you hate me?" I will ask these questions to everyone that I'll come out to. What people think of me has been so important—it is the padlock that has latched my closet door shut for all these years.

"Why would I hate you? I love you."

Love. Not hate. Well, it's official—I'm out, and I feel as free as the flags rippling through the wind atop the building. The door of my cage has flown wide open. With the fear exorcised from my body, the shivering has stopped and the chill that I've been feeling all morning has unclasped its icy grip. Begone, closet demon!

Danielle and I hurry back to our desks in silence, my revelation a belt cinching us together even tighter than before. I keep a firm hold of her hand until we get off the elevator. I apologize for dumping my shit on her, but she understands. I was her confidant in the months leading up to her leave of absence and all that suffering she went through. Now it's her turn to support me. She has held a mirror up to my face, prodding me to see the real Anil within, and for the first time, I am able to look at my reflection and not turn away.

"You, you, there's something a little bisexual about you!"

It's Christmas Eve 2007, a year and a half prior to my coming out, and Danielle and I are among the last few people left in the office.

Danielle is such an easy person to be around. There's nothing that I need to hold back, I don't have to be weary of the pitch of my voice, the sway of my hips, the content of my speech—I can just be me. This is where I seek refuge, in the comfort of nonjudgmental friends.

Leave it to Danielle to pull out a bottle of Bailey's from her purse—a brilliant purchase she made at lunch from the liquor store across the street. Our coffees are spiked—the perfect camouflage. Once three o'clock hits, our giggles are a routine occurrence, holiday or not.

After a few more rounds of boozy caffeinating and trading juicy office tidbits, I am feeling relaxed and loose. Danielle eyes me as I sit on my chair, sprawled back like my spine is made of Jell-O. An intoxicated grin starts to curl at the corners of my lips. I am such a cheap drunk.

Danielle sticks her index finger out, wriggles it in front of me, and declares in a joking tone, "You, you, there's something a little bisexual about you!"

I don't detect a hint of malice in her voice, and I am not offended in the slightest. Quite the opposite, in fact. Someone finally has the balls to make a comment to my face, and it's mama-bear Danielle with all her love and drunkenness rolled into one charming package.

But I'm still not ready, so I just smile and get up to give her a hug. I'm not the slightest bit bisexual, but kudos to Danielle for giving it a try. She has the appropriate tools at her disposal: alcohol and humour, but the revelation has to come from me.

I impose another sixteen-month sentence on myself.

"So, do you like boys or do you like girls?"

September 1997, ten years before Danielle wondered if I was bi-curious. My good friends, Seema and Freida, have taken me out for my twenty-first birthday at Broadway's. As we sit, waiting for our loaded plate of nachos, Freida asks her question. She could easily ask in the same breath what my thoughts are on Mariah versus Céline, but my sexuality is what she wants to clear up.

I stiffen in my chair and stare down at my cutlery. No one has ever dared ask me point-blank before. I look over at Seema, desperate for some backup, but she looks just as panicked as I feel, so I protect my inner gayby and lie.

"Girls?" I utter sheepishly.

Appeased with my answer, Freida carries on and starts to gab about our current work situation: we are all employed by the Gap—not just a store but a miniseries all in itself. And with that it's over, but not forgotten. I am in awe at how brazen Freida is. To her, me being gay or straight is no big deal, just a slight issue that she wanted to clear up before we demolished our nachos.

Anil, are you gay? Okay, cool! So, Ben totally looked at my boobs today and then rubbed my back. That's sexual harassment, right?

I wish my twenty-one-year-old self could be ready to say boys. I would spare myself a decade of heartache. A decade of lifeless existence. But I'm not. I am still full of self-hatred and repression. I find myself paralyzed by what-other-people-think syndrome. I think it should be a valid clinical diagnosis that requires treatment.

"The answer is boys."

April 14, 2009. I call it True Me Day. After having just come out to Danielle in the basement of our office building, I feel the instant urge to tell every single person I know, minus my parents. I know I'll have to tell them at some point, but in this moment of clarity, I can't harbour any more negative thinking. All I want to do is gush my truth out.

My cubicle no longer feels confining. My fingers zip across my keyboard as I write a message to Freida. She'll kill me for doing this over email, but it isn't like I can just pick up the phone and profess my gayness. Cubicle culture equals zero privacy. If you sneeze, someone two desks down will wish you *gesundheit*.

"Hey, I can't wait until after work, I have to tell you something," I write.

"Okay, tell me," Freida fires back almost immediately.

"Remember twelve years ago when we went to Broadway's and you asked me a question? Well, I lied. The answer is boys."

The wait for her response seems eternal.

"I know."

She knows?

"What do you mean, you know?"

"I know. I was just waiting until you were ready."

Wow. Freida, I adore the hell out of you, but you were too damned patient!

I pick up my cell phone and start texting my boyfriend, Jeff. Yes, I have a boyfriend. I have been living a second secret life that my friends know nothing about.

"So, I just came out to Danielle and then Freida!"

"What?????" Jeff replies.

"I think I'm gonna email Rania too, and I'm gonna meet Seema for lunch to tell her, and I'm meeting Nathan tonight for coffee. I think I'll tell him as well."

I feel like running out and confessing to strangers on the street, just for the sake of letting everyone in on my not-so-earth-shattering revelation.

"Okay, I'm so proud of you. I love you!"

He loves me.

Coming out is something that I've ultimately done for myself. For my sanity and well-being. But none of it could have happened without having Jeff in my life. I don't want to be in the closet with someone who isn't. That isn't fair. I want our relationship to blossom, but it can't with one of us rotting away. I've chosen to cut off the rot. I've chosen to bloom.

"When did your dad last have a heart check up?"

Fall 2009. I'm on the phone with my cousin, Shadna, who asks about my dad's health because she knows I will be telling my parents at some point in the near future. Her first concern is my dad and the reaction that we all fear might happen. Jeff is sitting next to me on the couch and can hear her every word. He pulls the phone out of my hand.

"Shadna! His dad will be fine. Trust me. Nothing is going to change."

What is he, psychic or something? The man has yet to meet my dad. I was raised by him, and so was Shadna, practically. I have the same concern as her—my father's reaction. What if I tell him and he has a heart attack and doesn't recover? What happens then?

Jeff thinks we are both being melodramatic and rolls his eyes at me.

"Look at how tight they are. Nothing will happen. It will take a few months, at most, and everything will be okay. And they'll *love* me. Parents always tend to love me for some reason."

Oh, Jeffery. How can you possibly foresee that? Why does my pessimism overshadow your pragmatic reasoning? I wish I could press the fast-forward button.

"You need to tell them."

December 2009. It's been a few months since I moved out of my parents' house and into my cozy (okay, small) downtown condo. Jeff has been staying with me since I moved in. He claims it's because my place has air-conditioning. Please, I better be higher up on his list than a reprieve from Ottawa's humidity! It makes no sense for him to be paying rent at his empty, hot apartment. It also makes no sense that I have yet to come out to my parents. I've moved out; there's a buffer. I need to rip off the last part of the bandage.

I bring up moving in together, officially.

"Listen, before you give up your place, there are two things that you need to agree to, or else we're done," I state as we sit in bed pondering the day's events as outlined on our smartphones. I put down my cell and turn to Jeff.

"Shoot," Jeff says, putting down his own phone.

"I want to get married, and I want to have kids."

"Kid."

"Sorry?"

"One kid."

"Deal."

"You know you need to tell your parents soon, right?"

Yes. "I know. I will. Love you."

"I know. And your parents will understand. They love you too. You guys have a super-close relationship, and you're their only son. It's going to be okay. But you need to tell them."

We give each other a kiss and return to our routine of scouring social media. Maybe I could come out to them via text message.

"Anil, we need to have a talk."

May 8, 2010. D-day. Winter has flown by, and I'm the happiest I have ever been, save for one major issue: my parents. My strict, religious, Indian parents. The main reason I waited until the age of thirty-two to come out. I don't want to hurt them. To disappoint them. To damage them. I'm all they have, their only son, their only child. Do you see how much pressure I've been exerting on myself? The weight of expectations.

If their fantasy for me as a newborn had ever come true, I would've been a dashing doctor, married to a gorgeous, successful woman from a good family, and we would have given them two perfect grandchildren. But here I am, thirty-two, single (at least that's what they think), unmarried, and the cause for copious amounts of sleepless nights, worrying, and whispers from nosy relatives.

My mother has had enough and is demanding some answers. Today is the day.

"Okay," I respond.

It's the day before Mother's Day, and I've come over for a visit. A steady stream of sunshine pours through the kitchen windows as we sit at their large granite island. I am perched on a stool with my mom sitting beside me. I didn't think that coming out to my mom would go quite like this. I was imagining more dread, convulsive tremors, maybe some shortness of breath. Why am I not freaking out?

"Anil, you're getting old. Your father and I are getting old. When are we going to have grandchildren? When are you going to get married?"

Shit. Knock me to the ground and pounce on my chest, Mom. Geez. She knows something's up. In the months that preceded my moving out, while I had just begun dating Jeff, I was never home, my constant yammering ceased, and curfews I had respected in my twenties (because I had no life) were ignored. Regardless of culture, no thirty-two-year-old should ever feel the need to come home at a decent hour.

I'm sure she knows that there's someone in my life. She just doesn't know which sex.

"Is she white? Is she Muslim? Is she...black? Is it Freida?"

Poor delusional Mom. She could list off any race, religion, ethnicity, or friend's name and still be dead wrong.

"Mom, you are so far off."

She turns away from me, pauses, and then asks *the* question.

"Are you gay?"

Like I did with Danielle, I've managed to get my mom to tell *me* and not the other way around.

"Yes."

Mom takes in the revelation. She doesn't cry. She doesn't yell. She doesn't pull me off the stool, drag me out of the house, and banish me from ever visiting again. She does none of the dreaded things that I foolishly imagined would happen when this moment finally came.

What comes next is a complete surprise.

"Why did you wait so long?"

Because I was expecting the worst.

She asks me when I knew.

"I always knew I was different, and you did, too, Mom."

"Yes, I always knew you were different, but I didn't know different meant *that*."

Yes, Mom, different did mean gay. I guess when you're a kid, you don't put a name on something that involves sexual orientation. To her, I was just her fabulous little boy who would belt out Diana Ross's "Upside Down" at the top of his lungs in the grocery store. My mom is my best friend, and her constant flow of selfless love, acceptance, and support has meant everything to me. Why *did* I wait so damned long?

After a few more questions, including the secondary reveal of having a boyfriend, I have to ask, "Are you mad at me? Do you still love me?"

"Of course I love you. You're my son. It's not your fault."

I have waited a lifetime to hear those words.

And then the kicker…

"I'm your mother. I should have known."

On some level she must have, but the secret should never have been hers to bear. She follows this by forcing what *used* to be my biggest fear in life to fruition. Not death, not taxes, not public speaking, but…"We need to tell your father."

My father. My Sikh, Punjabi father who used to instill fear into all my cousins and me when we were kids. As a child I was petrified of him. He worked very hard to provide for us, I never wanted for anything, and we traveled the world over. But disobey him and there would be repercussions. Corporal punishment was a routine practice in our household. I reviled his method of discipline, but it has ultimately shaped me into who I am today. As an adult, I have grown to love and admire him for his steadfast dedication to my mom and me, but he's the ultimate reason why I stayed in the closet for so damned long.

I try stalling. "Mom, it's Mother's Day tomorrow. Dad's birthday is on Monday. Do we really need to do this tonight?"

"Anil, I can't keep this from him. We have to tell him. Yes, tonight."

The afternoon drags on as we wait, me with dread, my mom with God knows what, until my dad comes home from work.

In the evening, when Dad finally gets in, he saunters into the kitchen, gives us a passing greeting, and heads straight to the cage of his beloved budgie, Nina, which hangs by the window next to the kitchen table. He opens the door and beckons Nina to jump onto his finger.

He takes her out, and she proceeds to welcome him with a few swift pecks on his lips. Nina is no ordinary budgie. He takes Nina's cage into the laundry room to change her seed cup and refresh her water. That bird must have been something special in her previous incarnation to have lucked out as my dad's pet.

After Nina's evening ritual, my dad goes upstairs to take a shower, comes back down, and eats his supper. All the while my mom and I sit like statues in the family room inspecting his every move. I have latched onto my mother's arm and will not let go. Normally she would try to pull away from me, but she has resigned herself. She knows I need that arm.

After Dad places his plate in the sink, Mom can't take it anymore.

"Kamal, come sit down. Anil has something to tell you."

I jab Mom's side and stare Dad down as he innocently walks around the island, into the family room, and eases himself into the loveseat. I avert my gaze to the TV over the fireplace. *The* moment has come. At last. And right before *Saturday Night Live*. At least everyone will be doing improv, so there's some consistency.

Who's on SNL? Everyone's favourite Golden Girl, Betty White! Oh, and Mom, Dad, by the way, I'm gay! Anyone want ice cream? We have pralines and cream!

Mom nudges me, and I nudge her back. I need a few more minutes. Thirty-two years and two minutes. She begins to tell Dad about our conversation earlier today. My heart increases its thumping as the shivering commences. Bodies know.

Tell your father. Shiver, shiver.

I never wanted to experience this moment. I would have rather lived a lie than disappoint this man. Now there's nothing left to hide.

It's Dad's turn to find out the truth. After Mom's exposé of the day's events, he sits there, stoic, pondering.

"So," he says in his lilting Punjabi accent, "Are you, the gay?"

I sure am.

I say yes, and he sits there in silence, taking it in. My dad has a tendency of taking long pauses before he speaks, more to translate from Punjabi to English than to make a point, but tonight those pauses feel interminable.

"Okay. Why did you wait so long to tell us?"

What? He's not mad? He's not yelling? He's sitting there with no imminent heart attack in sight, and he's not crying. There's no collapsing onto the floor writhing in the throes of a cardiac arrest.

My fear is what kept me caged, not my father.

"Because I didn't want to hurt you guys, to disappoint you."

"But we love you. You're our son."

And with that simple statement of acceptance, I know that everything will be okay. Now that I'm finally able to decompress, my tears rush forth. I weep choking, sniveling sobs and hold on to my mom, amazed at how astonishing my parents are and furious at myself for not giving them the credit they deserve.

Once the whimpering subsides and the three of us know that nothing has really changed, that I am still me, I wipe my face, get off the couch, and ask them if they want some tea. We then settle in to watch Ms. Betty White kill it on *SNL*.

Tomorrow may be a new reality for us, but tonight nothing has changed. There is no cage.

A Bit of a Shock

Jean-Pierre Vidrine

WHEN I WAS A BOY, I WASN'T BOYISH ENOUGH. OH SURE, I LIKED He-Man, Transformers, and the like, but I wasn't so keen on hunting, fishing, and most importantly sports. Perhaps I should back up.

My name is Jean-Pierre Vidrine. I was born in the small town of Ville Platte, Louisiana. My father and mother never married. He was a drunk who would not change his ways, so she left him before I was born. When I was about two or three years old, she married another man and had two more children with him: a boy and a girl. We lived in the even smaller town of Sunset, Louisiana, then. When I was nearing the age of seven, my mother's husband, the man I called Dad, was arrested. But that's another story. With her husband in prison, Mom took us three kids back to Ville Platte, where we lived with her parents. I was very confused by the whole matter.

Making friends was never easy for me. Of course, I was expected to befriend boys and eschew all things girly. That wasn't too difficult, as I had no real affection for the color pink or Barbie dolls. As stated above, I was genuinely into those appropriate "boy shows" of the time. But the boys on the playground expected more. Not knowing or caring about famous athletes or big sporting events branded me as a "weird kid" whose company the boys would tire of pretty quickly.

The kids in Ville Platte were far more aggressive and seemed a lot angrier than the kids in Sunset. Practically every day there was a fight on the playground with a huge crowd gathering around to watch. Here, my apparent deficiency in boyishness was met with more than puzzled glances. The fact that I was actually a pretty smart student was another factor in making me a target. With me not even having the slightest concept of sexuality at all, slurs like *faggot* were thrown at me.

I didn't even know what that word meant. The only gays I had ever known of were caricatures on TV and in movies, like Meshach Taylor's role as Hollywood in *Mannequin*. I had no idea that his over-the-top behavior was meant to indicate that he liked men. I actually thought he would be a pretty cool guy to know. He was certainly nicer than the bullies at school.

The closest person I had to a friend in those first few years in Ville Platte had to be kept secret. The reason was very stupid. He and I met on the school bus. I have absolutely no memory of that first meeting, but apparently his older brother who went to high school noticed. In his view I sat a little too close to his younger brother. Like I said, I don't really remember my first meeting with that kid, so I don't remember sitting too close to him. All I knew then was that he said we had to keep our friendship secret because his mother didn't want us to be friends. So we hung out together on the playground but sat separately on the bus.

Only years later, and still closeted from myself, did I put it all together. His brother assumed I was gay because I sat too close to him. He told his mother, who was afraid I would turn her young son gay, and she forbade him from hanging out with me. For the record, I don't believe I was attracted to this kid in that way. For that matter, I don't think I was attracted to anyone at that age.

Working out what had happened, and looking back on my youth and what must have been perceived of as my own girlish behavior, I reacted badly. Instead of being angry at the horrible people who judged me negatively for absolutely nothing, I became angry at myself. I began to overcompensate and express anger toward practically everyone. I was proud to have one of the nastiest tempers you would ever find in a high school student. I had few long-term friends, and plenty of people stayed away from me, just as I wanted it. Girlfriends came and went, with one relationship ending with such bitterness, it still pains me to think of it.

With great shame I admit that, whether prompted or not, I loudly espoused homophobic ideals. I built a wall of anger around myself to keep people away and to make it clear to everyone that I was *not gay!* When in the company of others, I would happily join in on the gay jokes and the rumors that so-and-so was a fag or a dyke...just to protect myself. I remember in one civics class, the teacher asked us about things we would look for in a presidential candidate. I must have had some encounter earlier that day that I do not recall now, but I definitely felt the need to make it clear to everyone that I was straight. I said that "not being a fag" was a quality to look for in a president. The teacher just chuckled at my statement. Does it say something about the time I lived in or about my school that I was not sent to the principal's office for that?

Outside of class, my acquaintances' rude jokes gave way to something that passed for rationalization. Probably prompted by more serious appearances of gays on the glut of daytime TV talk shows and Bill Clinton's efforts to allow gays in the military, we teens on the playground were convinced we had all the answers. No differently than the 'phobes do today, we regurgitated halfway thought-out "biblical" arguments against homosexuality. As for gays in the military, we vocally opposed the idea, though the best argument we had was to wince and shake our heads. Sometimes we would propose solutions for the "gay problem." The idea of conversion therapy was not something any of us were aware of, but we sometimes thought along similar lines. I remember joking that if I ever had a gay son, I'd buy him a hooker and tell him, "You're going to fuck this and like it!" Another guy proposed stringing gays up by their wrists and shoving large spikes up their asses so "they can get some enjoyment before they die."

For all of this horrible tough talk, I never actively tormented anyone I suspected of being gay. I definitely never could have lashed out with any sort of violence toward anyone. I am not saying this lets me off the hook. Though I was never a violent gay basher, I cannot say that my words were not overheard by someone who was. I worry that some terrible individual might have heard our remarks and found some kind of justification for anti-gay violence or activism.

In college, I was a mass of contradictions. While embracing academia and the arts, I still clung to homophobic ideas, though I tended to be much quieter about them then. I started college at Louisiana State University at Eunice, a sort of feeder school for LSU's main campus in Baton Rouge. For a time, I was the entertainment editor of the school's monthly newspaper, *The Bayou Bengal*. In one editorial I wrote, I blasted junky daytime TV talk shows. Recalling the article brings up more than just embarrassment. It invokes guilt. I could not resist, while blasting the type of guests on such programs, throwing out an attack at "flaming homosexuals." To this day I still wonder and worry about who might have read those words and took offense.

When I transferred to LSU's main campus, I made the incredible mistake of getting involved in party politics. Despite having eschewed the very idea of political parties since before I was even old enough to vote, I joined the Republican Party. This political involvement had me in the company of so many of the wrong people who influenced me in all the wrong ways.

Clearly gay rights are a hotly debated topic with candidates around the country today. But at that time, though an important issue, it was not talked about much by those candidates I came into contact with or campaigned for. I can only recall one candidate—I was not familiar with him, and I did not take note of which office he was running for—explicitly stating in his campaign ad that he voted against same-sex marriage. My guess is that he blew his entire campaign budget on that one TV spot.

Behind the scenes, away from the campaigns and in my own apartment, the homophobia was rampant. My friends and I met practically any mention of or positive portrayal of homosexuals in any media with sharp disapproval or outright anger. When playwright Tony Kushner was scheduled to make a special lecture appearance, I did nothing as an acquaintance tore a poster for the event down and threw it in the trash. When I ran into a friend I had not seen for some time, what began as a pleasant reunion quickly fell apart when she talked of going to see Kushner's lecture. I got loud and preachy. Though in the end we said polite goodbyes, I doubt she still thought of me as a friend after that.

All the while, though, little things were chipping away at my angry homophobic facade. The first was theater. My love of the stage and the arts introduced me to plays and movies where actors and characters were bending gender and challenging conventional ideas of male and female. In spite of myself, I found this attractive. The second was common sense. I would see people in life and on television making simple and logical arguments for gay rights and same-sex marriage. I would see their opponents ineptly quote the Bible and would wish for these people to just disappear. Remembering my high school days, I looked at my old companions with harder scrutiny. They would cough up the same religious arguments against gays, but how religious were they? These same guys were always boasting about indulging in underage drinking and meaningless sex (I wonder how much of the latter was true) yet dared to condemn a whole other group of people as sinful. The third thing that got me rethinking my anti-gay attitudes was something that I just touched on, and something people typically blame for the continued existence of homophobic attitudes: my religious faith.

I was born and raised Roman Catholic. In Mass and in Catechism, I learned about the stories of Jesus and to interpret the scriptures from an allegorical point of view. Jesus never said a word about homosexuals. In fact, he didn't exclude anyone in his message of how everyone should be loving everyone. The supposedly religious people I saw attacking gays certainly were not examples of loving people. These people were more concerned about following rules and conforming to their ideas of normalcy than they were with acts of compassion. Even people in my own Church and other denominations that were supposedly non-fundamentalist (not believing the books of the Bible to be the unerring word of God) would justify their bigotry with this or that quote from Leviticus. I am no Bible scholar, but you don't have to be one to see the obvious xenophobia that runs through much of the Old Testament. Those cherry-picked bits from it that the anti-gays love to throw about have their roots in ages-old politics more than actual faith. Recognizing this, I started to question my own faith. If I were truly a non-fundamentalist, how could I use the Bible or my faith to justify my anti-gay stance? And if that wasn't the basis for it, then what was?

The threads that had been holding my bigoted attitudes together were fraying.

Something weird happened during this time. It started while I was still at LSUE. It was Halloween time, and I wanted to dress up. At the time, I had a fascination with the story of the alleged and acquitted ax murderer Lizzie Borden. Combining this with my love of theater and shock rock resulted in me dressing up as a punk Lizzie Borden. I showed up at school in a black dress, wig, ghoulish makeup, fishnet stockings, and wielding a bloody rubber ax. The next year, the same loves and interests collided with my having seen the movie *Phantom of the Paradise* about five times. Drawing inspiration from the character in that movie named Beef, a flamboyant androgynous glam rocker, I showed up in hot pants, fishnet stockings, and a ripped-up T-shirt that didn't cover much. I trotted out this androgynous look (which I named Lizzie) a good number of times for years to come. Though at this point I was still hanging on to homophobic attitudes and identifying as straight. Do you see a contradiction here?

Then I met someone. A coworker of mine realized we had some common interests like science fiction and theater, so she suggested we hang out sometime. I was incredibly socially awkward at the time, and I wasn't sure why she'd reached out to me. Maybe I was even a little suspicious. Regardless, she and I started hanging out at coffee shops and going to movies together. We became great friends. Here, I reveal myself as something of an oblivious dolt, because I did not even realize at first that she was a lesbian who had been out and proud for years.

Somehow I just never noticed her pendant with two linked female symbols the first dozen times we hung out together. Finding this out caused something of an internal wrestling match for me. In spite of everything, I was still clinging to those anti-gay attitudes, probably more out of habit than anything else.

Finally, as it always should, good won. I reasoned that when people had labeled the idea of homophobia as hate, they were being perfectly accurate. I did not want to continue through life hating this woman who was such a great friend to me, let alone an entire group of people like her. I began dropping every anti-gay idea I had ever held. It was hard to hold on to such fear and hate when the object of them was no longer an object but a person I'd gotten to know very well. She and I became the best of friends, so much so that some of our coworkers thought we might have been more than friends. With her I went to gay and lesbian bars for the first time and started to develop an interest in gay culture, something I had always ignored before then. I even got a weekend job as a doorman at a lesbian bar.

Then I met someone else. A woman who had become a regular customer in the coffee shop where I was working asked me out. A day or two before we were to go out, I called her. During that first long conversation, she revealed to me that she was bisexual. She said that it was a rule of hers to just get that fact out in the open early on with a person she was to go out with. I admired her forthrightness and had no problem with her sexuality. We talked for hours that night and had a great time on our first date. Long story short, we got married a year later. My lesbian best friend was my best man. My wife graduated and got a job in Tucson, Arizona, and we moved.

Over the years gay and trans culture became more and more visible in the media, and I got more and more interested. My interest in the art of drag grew exponentially. I was convinced that these interests were one part academic, one part guilt, and one part simply appreciating the talent and gifts of people different from myself. While there was some truth to that, there was more.

I was in my thirties when the realization happened. Lying awake a few nights, I let my mind wander. Inevitably it would meander into the realms of sexual fantasies. Somewhere in there, I found myself thinking about more than just women. This startled me at first. Even though I had shrugged off bigoted ideas about homosexuality and bisexuality, suddenly finding that I could be attracted to more than just cisgender women was something I had not expected.

I kept quiet about it for weeks. In part this was to give the matter a lot of thought. A bigger part of being quiet about it was fear of what others would think, especially my wife. Though we had been married for about a decade at this point, and I had always been comfortable talking with my wife about anything, this was something I had never foreseen. I realize now how silly I was being. I was afraid of telling my bisexual wife that I in fact was also bisexual. One evening, after making love, during pillow talk, I finally told her. She raised her eyebrows for a second, then smiled and said that she had suspected it for a while. She was just letting me figure it all out for myself. I would guess that she'd had her suspicions for even longer than I had.

There is a bit of a question here. Was I bisexual all along, or did I change? Did the bullying and indoctrination I experienced early in life cause me to suppress a whole side of myself that I allowed myself to explore only after getting away from harmful influences? Likely. Or did getting away from bad influences and letting go of old angers and fears allow me to open up to different cultures and new experiences, bringing about changes in my perceptions of sex, gender, and what I deemed attractive? Also possible.

I may never know which of these actually happened, and it does not matter. Whether I was bisexual all along or my sexuality underwent the fluid change some like to talk about, I liked myself better this way.

Shortly after coming out to my wife, she asked me how I would handle this realization with other people. I said I wouldn't make a big deal about it. After ten years in a happy hetero marriage, I didn't really see the point. The point, however, presented itself to me before long.

Though I hadn't planned on telling anyone but my wife about my self-discovery, I couldn't help but be curious enough to search the internet for images and articles about bisexuality. Eventually I happened upon a few statements that sprung from that strange phenomenon my wife had told me about a few times: biphobia. I could not make sense of the fact that a number of gays and lesbians held such disdain for bisexuals, sometimes even asserting that bisexuality did not actually exist. Had these people not experienced such terrible bigotry themselves? Were they not aware that their own sexual identities were once treated as mental illnesses? The whole thing smacked of blatant hypocrisy.

In December 2012, we moved to Chicago. Eventually finding work as a theater usher, I found it easier and easier to be open about my bisexuality around my new coworkers who had become my new friends. Maybe there is just something about the theater. I even began wearing a bracelet with the bi pride colors: pink, purple, and blue. My friends and family in Arizona and Louisiana were still in the dark about it.

More and more I looked for articles and information about the bisexual community, and more and more I found biphobic statements. My own personal encounter with biphobia was fairly mild. A friend, unaware that my wife and I both identified as bisexual, casually commented that most people who say they are bi are just not confident enough about their sexuality. His implication, of course, was that they really are gay and are just confused. I was also seeing a lot of talk online about how so many people are afraid to come out as bi because they simply do not see any other bisexuals out in the world they can identify with.

On October 11, 2013, a little more than a month away from turning thirty-six, for National Coming Out Day, I made a snap decision. If anyone could be openly bisexual and not care what anyone said about it, it could be me. I got onto that omnipresent meeting place, Facebook, and with a shaky hand and a few tears in my eyes, I typed out a long coming-out statement. Bracing myself, I waited. To my surprise, no hate ensued. All of the comments that I expected about me being a sinner, a pervert, confused, and such never came. Though there were few conspicuously absent old friends, I got a lot of "Likes" and positive comments, some of them from unexpected sources.

So many of my anger issues seemed to disappear after I came out. Being open about my bisexuality just made me feel like a freer individual.

Looking back, I see how my coming out was a long process. First I had to let go of homophobia altogether. Then I had to be open to simply experiencing life and learning about people unlike myself. Then I had to be honest with myself. Then I had to tell my wife. Finally, I had to tell the other people in my life. Each one of these steps in the process was far more difficult than it should have been. The hardest part now is not looking back and wishing I had come out sooner, not beating myself up for the length of my journey. Plus, the guilt of my homophobic years still haunts me.

I cannot change the past, but maybe I can affect the present and the future. I hope that by being out and being visible, I help in making it just that little bit easier for other younger LGBT people to be honest with themselves and the people in their lives. Beyond that, I hope for a world that is accepting and loving enough so that there will eventually be no need for coming out—a world where simply being true to oneself is not a shocking revelation.

Epilogue: After being together for nearly a decade and a half, my spouse came out to me as genderqueer/transmasculine and is currently transitioning. We are still together and in love.

Casualties

David R. Gillespie

It was Sunday, March 24, 2002, when I finally came out publicly, unequivocally, at the age of fifty. There had been other coming outs during the course of my fifty years—to myself, to guys I'd fallen in love with or simply wanted to sleep with, to my mother—but on that day, there I was for all of Anderson, South Carolina, to see on the front page of the Sunday-morning paper. Above the fold. The week before Easter. In color. Now my high school classmates and teachers, my parent's friends, members of First Presbyterian Church where I'd grown up religiously would all know what they perhaps had suspected for a long time.

I am in a photograph, walking down the sidewalk of Anderson's Main Street, hand in hand with my friend Bryan. Above the photograph is the headline "Area's gay community looks for acceptance." In the story I am simply identified as "David, gay, a writer." But there is that photograph, and I'm unmistakable in it. Anyone who knows me knows that it is me.

I had pitched the idea of the visual to the reporter who was interviewing me for the story. She had been put in touch with me by a mutual friend, and we met one day for lunch. During the course of our conversation, I suggested the concept to her, which would, I thought, provide an eye-catching graphic for the story. I did not know at the time that it would run on a Sunday on the front page, above the fold.

While I point to that moment as my official public coming out, the process had started and stopped several times. The first start was when I was about fourteen years old. For a couple of years, I had been vaguely aware of my affinity for the masculine form: Tarzan movies were a favorite, and I developed a serious crush on Johnny Sheffield after he left the Tarzan franchise and started making the Bomba films. And then there were my mother's books on artistic anatomy (she painted portraits) which I would secretly pore through looking for male nudes. We all, I'm inclined to think, have a tendency to universalize our own experience at points, and I thought at the time that my attractions were no different than those felt by other boys. It took my friendship with a boy named Donnie to significantly register the notion in my youthful mind that maybe I was different.

The Boy Scout troop of which I was a member met at a local Methodist church. Donnie, whom I knew from junior high school, was also a member, and he would convince me to sneak off from the meetings in order to find a darkened Sunday school classroom in which to fool around, as much as two fourteen-year-olds in Anderson, South Carolina, in 1965 knew about fooling around. After all, we were both learning as we went along, as we explored what was for us in the uncharted world of sex.

Sex. My parents, for whatever reasons, never did have *the talk* with me. What I knew of sex (other than my experiences with Donnie) came from the verbalized experiences of my friends who talked about, and bragged about, their experiences and girlfriends. Seemed like they all had girlfriends. But it also seemed like they were speaking a foreign language to me when they would talk about them and their experiences with them. I had no girlfriend, nor did I particularly want one. I had no frame of reference. When they were out on their weekend dates, I was surrounded by guys at Billy Hong's Tae Kwon Do school. How I got there is perhaps revealing.

One Sunday afternoon, when I was in my "relationship" with Donnie, I had attended a youth group meeting at First Presbyterian

Church. I was standing on the sidewalk outside the church waiting for my father to pick me up when a car pulled up to the curb and a boy got out. I recognized him from my seventh-grade class at McCants Junior High. I really didn't know him. I knew he was older (he'd been in seventh grade a couple of times), but that was about it. I still remember what he looked like: tall, thin but muscular with a hard face, with blond hair combed up and back on his head. He had a very 1950s look as I recall, and he was from what my father called "the mill hill." He got out of the car, walked over, and said, "Hey, faggot!" He then proceeded to punch me in the face, sending me crashing down on the concrete sidewalk.

How did he know? I didn't think of myself as particularly fey. I never blew kisses at other guys or talked about how hot this one or that one was. Nobody other than Donnie knew. Or at least I thought he was the only one.

The next day I asked my father to sign me up for karate class.

Until the utterance of that boy who hit me, I had never heard homosexuality discussed, never heard a sermon on it—or sex in general for that matter. None of that was never mentioned in our local newspaper or on the television news. The unspoken, but understood, sexual ethic of my childhood was that you didn't do *that*, whatever *that* was, until you were married; but we all knew of those who were doing *that* with the occasional resultant pregnancy. But my parents and I didn't talk about it. I guess they figured I would learn what I needed to know by the time I got married, but they didn't count on that education coming from another boy.

I've often wondered why it took me so long to reach that public moment in 2002, there on the front page of the newspaper. I've often wondered how my life might have been different—not necessarily better, just different—had I not waited. I imagine it's a fairly common theme, not particularly unique to me, that wondering. We can look back on a number of aspects of our lives and wonder. What if I had done this? What if I had not done that? What would have been the outcome?

I can't help but think, in the absence of any empirical data that I'm aware of, that a lot of guys my age very often did what they could do, what they had to do, to mask their desires and affections for other guys. This is because of the places and the times in which we grew up and because our parents were who they were, especially our fathers, and because of the fear created within us.

In my case it was the 1950s and 1960s in what Flannery O'Connor famously dubbed, "the Christ-haunted landscape," the American South.

The small, drowsy Southern town of Anderson during that time was very much akin to those towns of popular imagination. Mayberryesque indeed. Its population was still relatively small, and you did, in fact, pretty much know everybody. At least you knew those who ran in your circles—and there were only a few circles.

The town itself was geographically divided between north and east neighborhoods and south and west ones, a division that was also economic. Much of the south and west parts of town consisted of neighborhoods that housed mill workers and their families. The south side was also the predominately black community. The white middle-class folks, the "professionals," lived in the neighborhoods of the north and the east. My father was one of those professionals, and it was he who played such an important role in my closeting.

Friedrich Nietzsche has a quote that begins, "What was silent in the father speaks in the son..." Nietzsche was presenting a palpable truth, one which resonates, I believe, with countless sons, especially those who are queer. Ray Gillespie was silent, and I've often wondered why.

I have an old photograph of him, sitting in the front row, first from the left. It's a picture taken many years ago, back when the world was aflame—the years of World War II. It's a portrait of his outfit. The faces are young—he was in his late twenties at the time—but there are a lot of miles in all of those eyes; miles that were accumulated in the cities and farmland of Europe, and in his case, miles traversed on the beaches and in the jungles of the South Pacific, particularly the Philippines where he served. I'm not sure of the date or location of the photograph, but he's wearing the insignia of the rank of major.

The men in that photograph were truly a great generation. No one can dispute that. I see them also in his Clemson College class of '39 annual: fresh faces full of optimism and excitement, young boy-men who, within a short two years following their graduation, found themselves in a global conflict that left many of them dead on the battlefield.

Was that the source of his silence? The horrors of war? I've found other pictures—old black-and-white ones he'd taken in the Philippines after the Battle of Manila. I'd be silent, too, if I had witnessed that kind of destruction—many dead on the battlefield or wounded in body and soul. Who would want to talk about that? But I cannot locate his silence, his distance, solely in that awful experience.

I have often wondered if it also had to do with the fact that after trying so many times to have a son of his own with his young war bride, he finally resorted to adoption. I was not, when you get down to it, his flesh and blood. I had been created by the union of two strangers. I was loved, yet always a stranger to him, often referred to at family gatherings as "Ray's adopted son." Was our biological strangeness complicated by my otherness? My queerness? There is a theory floated around every now and then that fathers of queer sons know this intuitively and, therefore, distance themselves. Did he know?

There are other descriptors that could be applied to my father. He was consumed by the Protestant work ethic of his time and his Scots-Irish upbringing. As a perfectionist he would often say things to me like, "Here, let me do that. I want it done right." He was given to a refined sense of justice and honor and duty. It was that which contributed, I believe, to his anger, which was rarely expressed but always smoldering, it seemed, under the surface. Perhaps that anger was kept in check by his quiet, unexpressed Protestant faith.

Raymond Gillespie. Boy-to-man soldier and officer who thought Douglas MacArthur walked on water. Stern, a quick disciplinarian with a volcanic temper, a man who saw the world only in black and white, right and wrong. Protective husband and, for the most part, silent, distant father. And I so did want him to be proud of me. He could never—I always thought, and still do—be proud of a queer son. It would be a private and public shame.

One night, when I was fourteen or fifteen years old, Donnie had come over to spend the night. We were to camp out in our tent in the backyard. My father came to the tent late that night to check on us before he went to bed and found us naked in each other's arms.

Typical Ray would have yelled and screamed and thrown things and beat my butt until I bled. I'd experienced that eruptive anger many times before and fully expected it then. But no, he didn't do that. He simply told us to get dressed and come inside, that what we were doing was disgusting and we shouldn't do it anymore, and that we'd talk about it later. We never did.

That event set the course for my understanding of my father's attitude toward all things gay. Disgusting. Shameful. Not to be discussed. That's what queer meant. That's what was behind that assailant's word, *faggot.* That's the picture of men loving men that was painted in my mind. I wanted to do it, and did when I could, but I always felt my father's stare over my shoulder, always felt terribly ashamed, always felt dirty and in need of cleansing and forgiveness.

My father's attitude was reinforced for me even in my forties, not long before he died. It had to do with my lifelong friend, Carleton. His father had served as the pastor of First Presbyterian Church for most of my youth and early adulthood and was also a good friend of my father's. Carleton's life had followed a somewhat similar trajectory as mine. After a failed marriage and very short career in the medical world, Carleton remarried and went to seminary to study for the Presbyterian ministry—as I had done. He first served a small South Carolina church, then became pastor of a larger, growing congregation in the foothills of North Georgia. I had returned home in 1990 to be closer to my parents. They were getting older and more infirm. His parents, too, had returned to Anderson in their retirement.

One day, word came to me via a neighbor who knew us both that Carleton had suffered some sort of breakdown and was now living in Anderson with his parents. I sent word to him that I would love to see him if he were up to it. Eventually he called and came over to my house.

During the course of our conversation, I shared with him my growing awareness of my gayness and told him of a lover I'd had while living in Columbia following my divorce. He then proceeded to share his story with me. Carleton had long understood himself to be a female and had sketched out what the future would hold in terms of living full time as a woman and undergoing hormone therapy and genital surgery.

Eventually my father heard about Carleton (now Carla), and his instructions to me were forceful and unambiguous: Don't hang out with Carleton. Don't be seen with Carleton. What he wants to do is disgusting. People will talk and think horrible things.

Social standing was always very important to my father, not so much in the sense of wealth or anything like that, but rather in terms of reputation, of what people thought of you. Beyond my father's simple inability to comprehend Carleton's desire to live authentically as a woman, the idea of his son associating with a guy who dressed up like a woman was simply out of the question. It would be a shame he could not bear.

If he could not bear that, I thought, then how on earth would he ever be able to come to grips with having a gay son, much less a publicly known one? Would I be shuffled to the side? Would I be disavowed? No matter, I was sure I wasn't going to tell him—or anyone he knew for that matter. Any coming out on my part would simply have to wait. I couldn't risk it.

Neitzsche, in the second half of his quotation, wrote, "…and often I found in the son the unveiled secret of the father."

Did that discovery of his queer son in that tent in our backyard bring to the fore, internally, some secret? Not that I think for a moment he was queer, at least not in the sexual sense. I don't at all think he lived anything other than an authentic life. But there in the backyard, so many years ago, something was, nevertheless, different—different in our relationship and his presentation in that moment of revelation.

The questions for me now at age sixty-three are: Had I ever convinced him I wasn't queer? Had I been out to him all along? How could he not have known?

Surely in addition to that backyard camping-out incident with Donnie, there were other signs: the noticeable absence of interest in females as I went through junior and senior high school, the young boy who would stand in front of the big console stereo faux-conducting Tchaikovsky's *Pathétique* symphony feeling every moment of its passion, the child who would spend hours in his room reading A. Lamorisse's *The Red Balloon* or painting plastic models. What about all of those photographs he took of me as a teenager, always, it seems, in the presence of another boy? What about the young adult son and his failed marriage, a failure prompted by a hidden love with another guy? How could my father not have known? Did he and my mother ever have those conversations? Did they ever pray for their son to turn out straight?

I often think of the word *casualties* when I consider my pre-out life. They are undeniable. A former wife. Children. Girlfriends I dated in an attempt to convince someone, even myself, that I wasn't gay. I am inclined to think the two greatest casualties of living that particular lie are my father and myself.

Walking down that street back in 2002, confirming what was probably a well-known secret, was the beginning of a process that continues even now. I'd like to claim that today, fourteen years after that newspaper article and photo appeared, and twenty years after my father's death, I am fully and totally out and proud. But the fact of the matter is there are still days when I hear his voice, days in which my outness waxes and wanes, days in which I'm still that embarrassed fourteen-year-old boy caught naked in a tent with another boy.

A Phone Call from a Closet

Clayton Delery-Edwards

IT IS 1985, AND I AM SPEAKING ON A PHONE. A LANDLINE, WHICH IS basically all that any but the rich and pretentious have in 1985. And I am in a closet. Not in *the* closet, but *a* closet. Literally. The one at the end of the hallway in the two-room dormitory suite that I share with three other graduate students. When the phone was installed, we got an extra-long cord, and whenever one of us wants privacy, we bring the phone into the closet that is used for no other purpose except that of a telephone booth. I am twenty-eight, and I have just had a fight over the telephone with my lover, Charlie (we still used the term *lover* then). I am upset because of the fight, but even more upset that I don't have anyone to speak to about it. I have left Louisiana to go to New York to work on a doctoral degree, even though it means Charlie and I will have to endure a long-distance relationship for several years. I did not know any of my roommates before the housing office assigned us to each other, and though we have lived together for several months, we have not really bonded beyond commonplace pleasantries. Now that I'm upset, and now that I need a counselor, or a confidant, or a shoulder to cry on, there isn't anyone.

With a surge of anger and resentment that one might charitably characterize as misplaced, I get angry at my siblings. At my oldest sister, who divorced her husband several years ago. At my younger brother, who met a woman, had a baby with her, married her, and divorced her—in that order—all in less than eighteen months. At my older brother, who was engaged to a woman, broke up with her, and almost immediately started living with another one. Whenever their relationships are on the rocks, they have been able to confide in my parents. Whenever their lives are falling apart, they have been able to pick up the phone and get some support from Mom and Dad. I've never been able to avail myself of such opportunities. Because I'm not just standing in *a* closet. I'm in *the* closet. At least as far as my parents are concerned.

I never liked the metaphor of the closet because the status of being *in* or *out* of it has always seemed clean-cut and absolute in a way that never corresponded to how most of the gay people I knew back then actually lived. In the seventies and eighties, we were all in with some people and out with others, and the condition of being out never seemed quite final. Some were out with their friends but in at work. Or they were out at work but still in with their parents. I can remember going to parties where men older and richer than I would discuss whether or not they were out to their cleaning ladies (as if anyone could keep that kind of secret from a cleaning lady!). And, of course, there were many who were out to their other gay friends but not to the heterosexual world. I'm speaking of gay men, but I suspect things were much the same for lesbians. A cartoon that ran in *Christopher Street* magazine in the seventies captures that moment in time perfectly: two women with sour looks on their faces are watching a third who waves at them as she walks down the street, her arm around a man's waist. One of the angry-looking women sneers to the other, "Her closet's got a revolving door."

In the midseventies, shortly after my eighteenth birthday, I started coming out to my friends, and, oh, what a laborious process it was in those days! First you had to identify the friend you wanted to tell. Then you had to maneuver to get him or her alone, without any chance of interruption. Then you had to orchestrate the conversation so that it was appropriate for A Very Important Discussion (sharing herbal tea helped set the mood; the right amount of alcohol was even better). Then you had to make The Revelation, saying something like, "I feel like you need to know this about me, because I really value your friendship, and I want us to be able to be honest with each other." At this point, the friend (if well chosen) would usually say, "I'm glad you told me, and I'll always be your friend," and mean it. And no matter how much the friends swore they would never tell anyone else, they always did, so you were never quite sure who knew and who didn't.

Coming out is so much simpler for me now. Much of it has to do with changing times, and much has to do with my four decades of experience in the process. These days, I operate on two assumptions: (1) everyone I'm in contact with already knows I'm gay (a pretty safe assumption after more that twenty-five years in a small town), and (2) the person I'm dealing with won't be shocked at hearing the news for the first time. If a new acquaintance sees the ring on my finger and asks about my wife, I just say, "I have a husband, not a wife. His name is Aaron." End of discussion.

But it was the beginning of the discussion in 1985. I had been coming out to my friends for the prior ten years, but I had not yet come out to my parents. I was using all the old, cowardly excuses that people used back then: They *probably* know, anyway. They just don't want to acknowledge anything. We're in a good place in our relationship, and I don't want to disturb it. You don't see straight people announcing to their parents what they do in bed, do you? Why should we?

Well, in response to that last question, when straight parents see their straight kids dating, getting engaged, getting married, having kids, and divorcing (not necessarily in that order), the straight kids are not, in fact, announcing to their parents what they do in bed, except in the most general terms. They are, however, announcing what they are doing with their hearts and with their lives. When straight kids want to celebrate an engagement, or try to understand a fight they've just had with a spouse, or mourn the death of a relationship, or share the birth of a new one, they can talk through the process with their parents. Closeted gay men and women do not have these options.

In 1985, after a fight with my lover, those conversations don't seem like options to me; they seem like necessities. So, having just hung up the phone with Charlie, and still in a/the closet, I punch in my parents' number, also long distance, and also in Louisiana. The phone rings twice, and my mother answers. I ask her to get my father to pick up the extension in the bedroom so I can talk to both of them at once. When Dad is on the line, I say, "There's some stuff going on in my life, and there's something really important that I need to tell you. I'm gay."

"Uh-huh," my mother says. "And?"

"And what?"

"What's the important thing you have to tell us?"

"I'm gay."

"Oh, honey," she says. "We've known that for years."

My father joins in. "Ever since you used to bring that friend of yours from college. He was *so* effeminate. What was his name?"

I get unbelievably frustrated. I have always suspected that they knew (or was it that I have always known that they suspected?), but I'm in the middle of The Revelation, and they're asking when I'm going to get to the important part.

And there really is a more important part. Telling them wasn't an end in itself; it was a means to an end. Telling them was supposed to clear the way so I could talk to them about the fight I am having with Charlie. And get their advice. And their comfort.

So I tell them, and they give me their advice. And their comfort. And I am grateful for it but still a little confused. And at one point I say, "You two don't know your lines. After I told you I'm gay, you were supposed to cry and scream and tell me that I'm ruining my life and that I've ruined yours."

My mother says, "Maybe we would have done all that ten years ago. But we've had a long time to get used to the idea by now. And we like Charlie."

When we hang up the phone, I feel a sense of relief for all kinds of reasons. I've gotten what I needed at that moment, and I've managed to avoid the tears and the fights and the recriminations that so many of my friends faced when they came out to their parents at the age of eighteen or twenty, or even thirty. It isn't for several more years, though, that I realize I managed to do something else: I managed to waste a lot of time.

I lost ten years of conversations we could have had. Not only serious discussions about who was important in my life, and why, and what my plans were, but much more casual ones about what Charlie and I had done in New Orleans the prior weekend (it was never anything very shocking). Or whether we should get a new comforter for the bed (not "his bed" or "my bed" but "the bed"). Or what was factoring into our decision about where to go on Christmas Eve, which for some years we didn't spend together, in part because to do so would be to make an admission. By the time I met my husband (not Charlie from 1985, but Aaron, whom I met twenty years later), these kinds of conversations with my parents were routine. I'm grateful for those twenty years, and for the six more we shared before my parents died, but I deeply regret the ten I missed. In retrospect, I have often thought that it would have been better to have come out to my parents at eighteen, and to have experienced the tears and recriminations, if doing so meant that we would not have avoided so many other topics for so long.

Here, as in so many areas, my husband was ahead of me. We were once sharing stories of coming out to our parents when Aaron said, "I remember being fourteen and realizing I was gay. I felt so unhappy and so alone! I had this huge burden that I couldn't share, and it was going to isolate me from everybody who was important to me until I could get up the courage to tell them. It was the worst forty-five minutes of my life!"

But coming out to my parents is not the end of my story. I went through a similar, though less emotionally fraught, process several years later at the workplace. I finished my doctorate thinking I would get a tenure-track position at a university but wound up accepting a job at a public high school. It is a specialized high school where day-to-day operations are much like those at a small liberal arts college, but it is a public high school nonetheless. When I had been a student, I was constantly exposed to works like *The Children's Hour, Tea and Sympathy,* and *Ladies of the Corridor,* which conflate homosexuality with preying on minors, and which suggest that even the flimsiest of rumors can end a teaching career. And though I'd known many gay and lesbian high school teachers, we were all afraid what would happen if the wrong parent or the wrong administrator found out we were gay. I did not, at that point in my life, know any K–12 teachers who were out in the workplace.

So at first I tried to stay closeted—just at work—but that enterprise was doomed in a small school and a small town. In the first place, it quickly began to interfere with my relationship with my colleagues. People who are against LGBT equality in the workplace often suggest that somebody who "makes the choice" to be gay should just keep it to him- or herself, often adding, "You shouldn't be talking about your sex life at work anyway." But of course, this misses the point much in the same way as my friends and I had several decades ago, when we said, "You don't see straight people announcing to their parents what they do in bed, do you?"

Of course people shouldn't be discussing private sexual practices in the workplace. But in most instances, the majority of people in a workplace will be straight, and they will be forever casually making references like, "My wife and I went to Florida last summer," or "My boyfriend and I hate that new restaurant downtown," or "My fiancé and I are thinking of an outdoor wedding." To remain closeted on the job is to forever edit and censor one's speech, even in the most casual of interchanges. People can tell when someone is holding back. The result—at best—is a chilly social distance. At worst, it breeds mutual distrust.

But more important than not serving me well in social situations, trying to remain closeted at work, I soon realized, was doing the students a bigger disservice. In the first place, adolescents have finely tuned gaydar, so I wasn't keeping anything secret that they didn't already know. In the second place, many of them were wrestling with their own LGBT identities and looking for an adult to confide in. By keeping silent, I was not only withholding support they needed (and support that I would very much have appreciated at their age), but I was also reinforcing the message that their adult lives would be ruled by secrecy and fear.

It is the spring of 1994. I have a student I'll call Barbara who is emotionally and sexually confused. For several months, she has been seeking me out during office hours. She introduces works such as *Cabaret* or *A Streetcar Named Desire* into our conversations. I am not teaching these works, but she still asks me questions about the gay characters and themes, allowing us to talk about the broad issues without either one of us making a personal admission. There is always a sense of desperation under her questions, a nervousness that many of the teachers and counselors sense, and that seem particularly pronounced in her dealings with me (though that may be my own paranoia). One day she comes to my office and asks, "Have you ever felt guilty for having a penis?"

"What did you say?"

"Have you ever felt guilty for having a penis?"

The question is so unexpected, taking me by such forceful surprise, that I forget, for a moment, how inappropriate it is. "No, Barbara," I say, "I have felt guilty for many things in my life but never about my plumbing."

"I was wondering," she said, "because in *Kiss of the Spider Woman*, there's a gay man who says that he's always felt guilty for having a penis. And I was wondering if other men felt that way."

I look at my watch. Class doesn't start for another ten minutes, and it's only a three-minute walk, but I say, "Got to go. I'm running late." I leave my office, making a quick detour to see a counselor, who listens to my story about Barbara. The counselor says, with almost comic understatement, "Barbara has been working through some issues." The counselor promises to have a conversation with Barbara about "boundaries."

But, of course, my feelings about my penis were never really what Barbara was asking about.

This is reinforced a week or so later. At a social event hosted by the school, Barbara corners me again and says, "I need to ask you a personal question."

I look around and identify several other students within earshot, one of whom is openly eavesdropping. "Sorry," I say, "that's off limits."

Barbara clearly isn't expecting that answer, so after a moment's hesitation, she says, "Okay, then, I'm going to tell you what people say about you. They say you're gay. Is that true?"

I take another glance around. The person who had been openly eavesdropping is still doing so. "Sorry," I say, "I'm not going to respond to that."

The memory of that moment makes me cringe. It's a reaction I still have when an actor, singer, or politician refuses to address rumors that he might be gay. The calculated nonresponse is the most blatant admission possible (no straight person would respond in that way), and it's all the more blatant because of the internalized homophobia it reveals.

I later apologize to Barbara—after she graduates—and I never quite stop second-guessing my interactions with her. She has clearly violated all kinds of limits in her interactions with me, but however improper her behavior has been, it has had a certain core honesty which my own has lacked.

So starting in the fall of 1994, I throw *The Children's Hour* and *Tea and Sympathy* out the window and start playing the game by a different set of rules. In the next twenty years, many LGBT or questioning students come to me, sometimes asking for advice in dealing with their sexuality itself and sometimes asking for advice in dealing with a parent. I give them the advice and do so as an openly gay man. At various times, I sponsor both the school's AIDS Awareness organization and its Gay-Straight Alliance. I sometimes teach independent studies in LGBT literature, and I lecture and publish on LGBT issues. These days, if students ask in class what I did over the weekend, I say, "Aaron and

I went hiking," or "My husband and I worked in the garden." Aaron often accompanies me to school events, and when we have students over to our house, we never pretend to be "roommates." If any of the parents, faculty, staff, students, or administration don't know I'm gay, they simply aren't paying attention.

As much as I would like to historicize the complications of coming out to parents or colleagues, as much as I would like to think that these issues were solved at some point in the nineties, I know that the problems are still very real. The 2015 Supreme Court ruling on marriage equality, following several years of favorable rulings at the state level, has resulted in some people taking one step forward only to have to take one step back, with gays and lesbians finally being able to marry their chosen partners, only to be fired for doing so.[1] A 2009 study by the Human Rights Campaign suggests that over 50 percent of LGBT people are still in the closet at work. A 2013 Pew Research Poll found that over 40 percent are still not out to one or both of their parents.[2]

I certainly understand the fear of rejection in coming out to parents, having been there and lived through that. I was fortunate in the reception I received, but a positive reception was never guaranteed. I've known people who have been cast out and disowned by their families. Most have eventually achieved a truce. Others haven't, but they've at least been able to escape from the shadow of constant fear. In the years before I met Aaron, I was dating pretty actively, and I met people who were in their twenties, thirties, or forties who deliberately chose

---

1. See Samantha Tata and Ted Chen. "Gay Teacher Fired After Marrying Longtime Partner." *NBC News, Los Angeles.* August 2, 2013. Web. November 24, 2014; See also Stephanie Farr. "Michael Griffin, Gay Pennsylvania Teacher, Fired for Obtaining Same-Sex Marriage License." *Philadelphia Daily News.* December 9, 2013. Web. November 24, 2014.

2. See "Degrees of Equality: A National Study Examining Workplace Climate for LGBT Workers." *Human Rights Campaign Foundation.* September, 2009. Web. November 24, 2014; see also "A Survey of LGBT Americans Attitudes, Experiences and Values in Changing Times." *Pew Research.* June, 2013. Web. November 24, 2014.

out-of-the-way restaurants for dinner, or who would even insist upon meeting me in another city, because they didn't want to be seen publicly with another man. Once, during a lunch date, I offered assistance to a man who was getting ready to go to his sister's house to help her move some furniture. My offer threw him into a panic. "I can't bring you with me," he said, his voice quavering. "How would I explain who you are?" Another man became angry with me because we had ordered room service in a hotel and I refused to hide in the bathroom when the bellhop brought the food. These dates were typically last dates; having gotten to a place in my life where I was no longer looking over my shoulder in fear, I wasn't about to do it for anyone else's benefit.

I am more sympathetic to people who are afraid of losing their jobs, but even then, my sympathy has its limits. I was fortunate to find a gay-friendly workplace, but I would not have remained in a hostile one. People sometimes say, "I don't have a choice. I need this job!" But does that really hold up? Aren't you making a choice by allowing the boss to dictate the terms of your private life? If you're doing good work and helping the company achieve its mission, will someone really fire you if you say, "my boyfriend," or "my partner," instead of, "my roommate"? And if the boss *does* fire you, do you really want to be in the business of helping a bigot to prosper? Is this job *really* the only one available?

I'm especially perplexed by LGBT people who work from inside the closet for churches, religious organizations, or political organizations that are hostile to LGBT equality. In my mind, they are complicit in perpetuating the homophobia. I've heard some people explain their actions by saying that they're working for change from within, but it's never been clear to me how silent acquiescence amounts to working for change.

From time to time, Aaron and I have encountered some bigoted service providers or neighbors. It took us awhile to realize this, but we have ways to push back, and we have leverage! When we bought a house in 2014, we insisted that the records describe us as married, even though Louisiana did not, at that time, recognize the marriage. The sellers, loan officers, and attorneys all wanted the sale to go through, so they all agreed. More recently, we applied for a car loan. The first loan officer we dealt with either could not or would not wrap her head around the fact that we were two men who were married—to each other! After correcting her several times, we went with another loan provider, and we let the first one know why. Sure, it was uncomfortable when the eighth-grade boy next door called Aaron a "homo" but not nearly as uncomfortable as it was for the boy—and his parents—when Aaron confronted them with what he had done. We call out bigots and bigotry when we encounter them because we want to live on our own terms—not on theirs.

And the result is that we've lived very well, with a large and active circle of friends, many of them straight. After working for over twenty-five years in a public school, I'm in a position to retire at a comparatively young age. The world has changed a great deal since 1985, and I have changed as well. There really is no longer a reason to make any kind of phone call from any kind of closet.

A Taste of Southern Comfort

Patrick Cornelius

I CAME OUT AS A LESBIAN AT AGE TWENTY-TWO. AT LEAST TO MY FRIENDS. For years I lived two different lives: in the closet to most family members and some work colleagues, and out of the closet to those outside those circles. I never blatantly lied about who I was; I just never talked about my personal life. I always lived with "friends" or avoided answering detailed questions about who I was dating. My family quietly accepted me by not asking questions or by living in denial…and at the time that worked out for all of us.

There were lots of times I'd wished I could go to my mom for relationship advice, but I was so afraid she would disown me for being gay that I just dealt with things either on my own or through the help of friends. One of the hardest things about not being out to my family for all those years was living through an abusive relationship. Throughout the five years I spent in that relationship, I was so scared of my family's rejection, as well as being embarrassed about allowing myself to be stuck in such a relationship, that I never told them about that experience.

Fast-forward to age thirty, when I finally came out to my mother. The thing about my mom is that she has lived most of her life in denial about a lot of things. Anyone else who knew me wouldn't have been surprised by my coming out, but my mother insisted she never had any idea. In preparing to tell her, I had built up all kinds of scenarios in my head of how horrible things were going to go down. In the end, my mom told me I was her kid no matter what and that she loved me. Mind you, she didn't agree with my lifestyle, and she told me the Bible said it was wrong so it must be wrong, but that didn't change her love for me.

Throughout my years living as an out lesbian, I always felt like that label didn't quite fit, but I went with what I saw in my community and figured I was just a "butch lesbian." However, I hated that label as well, so most of the time I just said I was gay. I just knew I was *me*, the person who didn't really fit into a neat box and just lived my life.

I loved my lesbian/sporty dyke community. It was a major part of my identity for many years. During those years, I loved being around and with women, but I also started realizing my attraction to men. I wrote this off as non-sexual crushes, because I figured as a gay woman, that just wasn't allowed.

When I was in gay clubs or around gay men, I'd frequently be hit on and mistaken for a guy. It started to become a game to me, and I enjoyed going out and seeing how often this could happen.

Several years later, I also noticed I was expressing myself more and more in a masculine manner. It was never a conscious decision; it just evolved. In my everyday life, I was being called *sir* regularly. Sometimes, depending on who I was with, I'd correct the person. Other times, mostly when I was alone, I'd just go with it.

In 2005, the Logo TV channel came out. That became one of my favorite channels. For those who don't know, it was the first commercial LGBT channel on TV. One night a documentary called *Southern Comfort* came on. This show was about a trans man in the Atlanta area who had gotten cervical cancer and was dying because he couldn't get a doctor to work with him because he was trans. The documentary followed him and his friends as they planned and then attended one of the largest annual transgender conferences in the country.

After I watched the show, there was a spark in me. Many things in my life started to make sense. I had to learn more about this conference and the people who were attending, as well as their journeys. At the time, I was living in Birmingham, Alabama. The conference was in Atlanta, Georgia—a mere two hours away!

I had just missed the conference for that year, but I started reading as much as I could about what it meant to be transgender. I thought there was no way I could ever do something like transitioning, but the questions that were bubbling up within me were both exciting and terrifying. The thought that this was not for me paired with the new thought that it *was* me made me pretty sad. I thought for sure I was too old and too far into a career to even consider transitioning. I was so concerned about what other people would think.

The following year, I secretly attended the conference. I lied to all my friends and just said I was visiting other friends in Atlanta. It was the most amazing experience. I met so many awesome people and learned so much about transitioning. But still I felt there was no way I could do it.

Later that year I met a woman and began a three-year relationship with her. While I initially thought I was happy, I quickly grew upset with myself for breaking a promise to myself that I would take time away from dating to do some soul-searching. Sometime during the first year of our relationship, I tried approaching the subject of me feeling male and wanting to consider transitioning, but my girlfriend shut me down and made me feel ridiculous. I bottled up my feelings for the final two years of our relationship and never brought the subject up again.

Those last two years were miserable for me. I was already a workaholic, but to avoid the situation, I spent more and more time at work. When we broke up in August, the first thing I did was sign up for the Southern Comfort conference held that September. I was ready to more closely examine transitioning, and this time I wasn't going to let anything get in the way.

This time around, I met several gay trans men at the conference. Again, a whole new world was opening up. I had no idea there was such a thing as gay trans guys! I also learned the difference between sexual orientation and gender identity and realized the two were completely different.

While I was feeling a lot more comfortable with who I knew I had been for so long, I still couldn't imagine myself living full time as male. Even though I had met so many people successfully living as their authentic selves, I was sure that wouldn't work in my world.

A few months after that conference, I accepted a job in England. Living and working in England was exactly what I needed. It gave me a chance to be away from people I knew, meet a whole new trans community, and spend time really figuring myself out.

Through a combination of therapy, workshops, and a great community full of resources, I decided I was ready to transition. On September 12, 2012, at forty-three years old, I started taking testosterone.

Upon returning from England, I chose to move to Portland, Oregon. I was ready to start a new life and a new career, and I had heard there were tons of resources available for transitioning there, that it was a queer Mecca.

Since I began my transition, I've been on quite the journey…physically, emotionally, sexually, and mentally. I went through the usual trans stuff—name change; ID change; school, work, financial document changes; coming out to family and friends; stressing about health care and surgeries; living as stealth in some situations and not in others. I've also embraced my sexuality and become comfortable with the fact that I'm allowed to be attracted to whomever I want.

I began exploring my attraction to both cisgender and trans gay men. I navigated the world of online dating, NSA hookups, video stores, and people flaking out on you when they say they want to meet. I also started navigating connections with cis men and my dysphoria around my outside body not matching what's under my clothes—an exploration that has been both exciting and, at times, depressing. While I occasionally get frustrated, I know that everything that has happened so far in my transition is supposed to happen. It's all part of my learning process and journey.

One thing that I never considered when starting my transition was how my race and my gender would intersect. I had no idea what the effect of being seen as an African American male in America would have on me. I'm not sure what world I was living in before, but I was so oblivious.

I now notice not only women's fear of men in general, but also some white women's greater fear of black men. I also notice how the fear of and hatred for black men is so woven into our American culture that many people don't even realize how pervasive it is. I have learned to become acutely aware of my surroundings: I take my hood off when walking into a store or onto the bus no matter how cold it is; I try to stay in well-lit areas when walking at night; I'm super-observant of the speed limit. My work as a funeral apprentice requires me to visit homes late at night for body removals, often in rural areas. I am constantly worried that I'm going to go up to the wrong house and get shot or have the police called before I have an opportunity to even identify myself. I'm also constantly worried that I'll mistakenly be arrested and then have to deal with not only being a black man, but a black trans man, in our criminal justice system. (For the record, I've never had any interaction with the police in my life.)

Before transitioning, when I was seen as a black woman, I never worried about any of the situations of white-on-black violence we see in the news. I never considered what I'd be going through as a black man after my transition. I have to be honest, the reality of it all really fucked with my head! If there was anything I could change about my journey, it would be to eliminate this fear, this stress, this system of hatred and violence that haunts me and those like me on a daily basis.

My journey has had and continues to have its challenges: I struggle daily with dysphoria; I mourn the loss of my lesbian community; I battle with my family to understand and respect my transition; I worry about starting a new career as a middle-aged man; I stress about being outed as trans in a very conservative industry. But I take it all in stride. I know it's all part of the process of getting to live as my fully authentic self. It took me almost four decades to get to the place where I can say I'm that authentic man, but it's a journey I'll never regret.

Owner's Manual

William Dameron

SCOTT REACHED ACROSS THE TABLE, GINGERLY PLUCKED A FRENCH FRY from my plate, and cooed, "Oh, I really shouldn't eat this. A girl has to watch her figure." He batted his eyelashes, which I suppose he thought was adorable, and then asked, "Am I just horrible?" A mudslide that destroyed an entire neighborhood was horrible. A plane that crashed in a terrific fireball was horrible. Stealing a single French fry from your date's plate was not horrible.

"Why don't you take the rest?" I asked. My appetite had vanished.

"I couldn't." He smiled and then glanced sideways at me. "Well, maybe just a few."

In his profile photo, Scott had looked blond, complex, and impish. On the phone, his voice and personality had been a mixture of Philip Seymour Hoffman and Katharine Hepburn. There was a certain *je ne sais quoi* about him.

"I just arranged a birthday *brunch* for my friend," he said, rolling his eyes at the word *brunch* as if to say it had come to *this*, then continued, "I simply cannot stay out all night like I used to.

"I'm such a bitch," he said, swatting my hand and then letting his fingertips rest a moment too long. My hand retreated like a dog walking backward.

In person, Scott was not a mixture of anything. He *was* Katharine Hepburn. In short, he was simply not my type. He was Spencer Tracy's type. I wished that I could tell him this, but I was new to the dating scene and had not learned how to be candid.

"You know, you should change your profile photograph," he said.

Scott had learned how to be candid.

"Oh, is there something wrong with my picture?" I asked.

"There's nothing wrong with it per se, but you should open up that kisser and let us see those pearly whites. You look so serious in it. Well"—and then he looked at my expression—"like now."

That is when it struck me how deceptive the thumbnail profile photographs were. From a distance many men looked really attractive, but when you expanded the photos, you could see all of their flaws. The eyes were too close, or the teeth required work, or there was something just not quite right about the way all of the parts were put together. And then there were the photographs that looked too good. The lighting was soft and reminiscent of a Parisian sunset in autumn, the skin flawless and the features chiseled like Roman gods. These men were too beautiful to be in love with anyone other than themselves, or else they had become extremely proficient in Photoshop, in which case they were still in love with the image of themselves.

When Ray's calls had begun to dry up, I could not shake the feeling that I had somehow failed, that there was something wrong with me. He was the first man I dated after coming out, and I couldn't believe my good fortune in finding who I thought was Mr. Right on the first date. I became that sixteen-year-old girl obsessively checking for new text messages. This continued until one night over dinner when my brother Chuck asked if I thought Ray was controlling. I put the pieces together. All of our dates were on his terms, and sex was a lesson in obedience: sit, stay, roll over, and beg. I was like his dog, Molly, who desperately wanted his attention. He made her sit on the carpet across the room as he poured the dog food into her bowl. This was all the proof I needed to shift the blame. There was nothing wrong with me; it was him.

I made my dating profile viewable again. After forty-four years in the closet and three months with Ray, I was eager to find the one. He was out there, and I didn't want to waste any time. What if he was just beginning to date someone else? What if I'd missed my small window of time? What if I had given up everything—my children, my home, and my life—to be alone forever?

"Why don't you just take a break?" Chuck asked.

We had begun to talk to each other once a week by phone, comparing our searches. Like many adult siblings, we reverted to our adolescent personas when talking to each other. There was a slight edge of competition, but now that we played for different teams, I was filling him in as I made my hour-long commute from Franklin to Waltham after work. He seemed just as eager as me to find someone. When one dating site began to run dry, he would crank up a profile on another one.

"The guy who is looking for women on Plenty of Fish is telling me to take a break?" I asked.

"It's a free site," he replied.

"You get what you pay for," I said and then added, "Just the name of that site creeps me out, like you're putting a worm on a hook and trying to catch your next meal."

"Well—" Chuck began to reply.

"Don't even go there," I said.

"I'm thinking of joining the gay men's swim team," I said. My youthful years of competitive swimming next to sinewy, barely clothed bodies had transformed the scent of chlorine into a sort of aphrodisiac.

"That's cool. What's the name of the team?"

"Liquid Assets."

"Oh Lordy," he replied.

Instead of taking a break, I became a joiner, trying to cover all of my bases. I signed up for the Boston Gay Professionals Meetup Group and the inquirers group at Trinity Episcopal Church, and attended the Gay Men's Domestic Abuse Project Halloween fund-raiser dressed as a Boston Red Sox player.

"Are you a tight end?" inquired a man with a lamp shade on his head.

"No, tight ends are only in football," I replied as I attempted to put my drink down on a small side table before realizing that it was attached to him.

"Not in your case," he said, his eyes shifting downward, below my waist.

"What are you?" I asked.

"A night stand," he said and then added, "Get it? One. Night. Stand."

He gave me his card and asked me to join him and his husband (who was dressed as a cowboy or maybe Howdy Doody) in Jamaica Plain, where we could "explore each other's bodies." I had enough trouble navigating the boundaries of my own body, let alone three. I threw the card away.

When those avenues did not turn up anything promising, I attended the gay fathers support group in the basement of a Unitarian Universalist church in Waltham. When I felt blue after returning from a weekend visit with my daughters, I'd gather with the other sad men, sitting in uncomfortable folding metal chairs, passing the talking stick around as, one by one, a nervous guy would tug at his collar and stammer through the week's trials and tribulations, recounting his "God knows I tried" story. In retrospect, we should have used that stick to beat some sense into our self-pitying heads.

One night, when the talking stick landed in the lap of a good-looking new guy, the room of gay fathers took notice. He was broad shouldered and cocky, and wore a dirty-blond crew cut and a New England Patriots sweatshirt. He was shaped like a refrigerator, all hard angles, and coolly confident. He introduced himself as Greg.

"I'm not a father," he said. The gathering of enraptured men replied, "That's OK."

"I've never been married," he confessed, and the crowd responded in unison, "Good for you!"

"When I told my mother I was gay, she said you must get it from your father," he said. The men erupted into such applause, you would have thought that God had just farted.

When the meeting ended, word went around that we should all walk over to the bar across the street and continue the support over a libation of our choosing, giving us the chance to get to know one another in a less formal setting. When I walked out the church door, Greg was leaning against the frame, checking his phone. He asked if I was joining the other men. When I told him that I thought I just might, he said with a wink, "Then I guess I'll go too."

At the bar, I sat between Greg and a man from the group named John. When I overheard Greg drop an *r* at the end of a month, I mockingly repeated it, "Octobah." He leaned in, brushing his leg against mine, and said, "I think you're making fun of me." He continued to flirt by teasing and nudging me with a shoulder and lightly punching me in the arm. If we were in the locker room, he would have popped me on the ass with a rolled up towel. When I asked him what he did for a living, he told me he was a box salesman, which I found exceptionally fascinating.

"Corrugated cardboard boxes?" I asked, doe-eyed.

"Yup."

"How interesting," I replied. "Tell me more."

I was smitten.

When the bar started to thin out, Greg asked if I had a business card. I searched through my wallet looking for one. When I came up empty-handed, I whispered to John, asking if he had a pen and something to write on. He sighed and said, "He just wants your phone number." I offered my number, which Greg then keyed into his phone.

He called me from his car on the way home and told me he was looking for something long term. "How wonderful," I said, as I was looking for exactly the same thing. We exchanged emails and planned to meet up on Sunday for a bicycle ride around the Wachusett Reservoir in western Mass, near his home. Later that week, I bought a bike.

In between that first meeting and our first real date, he traded emails and texts with me, which I found to be quirky and cute. At the end of each day, he would send a text, "I hope you had a good day."

"This might be the one," I told Chuck, who had heard this from me once or twice before.

"Can I give you some advice?" he replied.

"Of course. I trust your experience."

"Don't have sex with him," he said. "Wait to see if there is an emotional connection before you make a physical one."

"Absolutely," I replied.

Greg's house was a cute one-story bungalow on the edge of Worcester with a front porch that stretched the width of the house, sheltered by a low-slung roof. The kitchen had a retro 1950s look with bright colors, orange-and-green–painted cabinets, period appliances, and decorated with kitsch. The kitsch was just enough, not too much: a cat clock with bobbing eyes and swinging tail and a cow-shaped creamer. On the wall in the living room was a black-and-white photograph of a graceful ballet dancer.

"That's my mother," Greg said as I stopped in front of the picture.

"She's beautiful," I replied.

"She always said that having children ruined her career," he said.

"What about your father?" I asked.

"We don't talk much."

"Oh" was all that I could muster up as a reply. I turned my head to look at the rest of the room. "Your house is adorable."

"Would you like to see the basement?" he asked.

Most people would begin to question their better judgment at this point. The fact that I met Greg at a gay fathers support group and that he had never been married nor fathered children? Fine by me. That I had known him for less than a week and he wanted to show me his basement? Perfectly safe. What really should have concerned me was my lack of sense, but I was blindsided by his charm.

"Sure, I'd love to," I replied.

We walked into the kitchen, and I followed him through the door to the basement, which was unfinished and had cement floors and exposed rafters. It was a cellar like any other except for the two rows of washing machines, probably fifteen in total. The machines against the wall were lit with overhead lights spotlighting their varying hues—blue, avocado green, burnt orange, all restored to their original vintage glory.

"You collect washing machines?" I asked instead of simply turning toward the steps and walking out the door.

"Yup," he said. His eyes were lit up like a boy discovering shiny boxes beneath a Christmas tree. He pointed to the row in front of the illuminated ones. "Those are a work in progress."

I looked closer and could see PVC pipes and electrical cords snaking behind the machines next to the wall. Not only were they restored, but they were all operational. At the end of the row of machines, huddled in the corner next to a small pile of parts, sat a single white dryer, separated from the others.

"You don't collect clothes dryers?" I asked.

He screwed up his face and asked, "Why would I collect those?"

"No, of course," I said, shaking my head. I decided to find his hobby charming, the most normal and natural thing in the world.

"Are those dishwashers?" I asked, pointing to a couple of machines on the other side of the room.

"I'm just dabbling in those, but they really don't do it for me."

He led me back upstairs, and when we passed his bedroom, he pointed in and said with a grin, "This is where all the magic happens. I'll just change into my shorts."

When he dropped his pants, I felt voyeuristic and looked away, but not before I saw him in his underwear. They were the type I'd worn when I was a little boy, white briefs with a thin orange-and-blue stripe on the elastic band. They were designed more for coverage than sex appeal. My mother had written each of our names on the inside of ours with a permanent marker. I wanted to peek inside his briefs, for multiple reasons, but in large part to see if "Gregory" was written in blue ink on the label.

After a bike ride through a sun-speckled path beneath a canopy of orange and yellow leaves, we returned to Greg's house and he offered me a beer. While sitting next to each other in the living room on the leather sofa, he told me he believed in being there for someone in good times and bad times. That love became better and deeper over time with one person, and that he wanted to give all of himself to someone. He did not believe in casual sex.

"But hey, I'm a guy. I like sex, but it's just so much better when you are committed to someone," he said with a shrug.

Where have you been all of my life? I thought.

"I've had a few long-term relationships, the most recent was with a guy in New Hampshire, but he couldn't make the time to see me," he said.

"I'll always make time for the right guy," I said, glancing sideways at him.

He then locked eyes with mine and said, "It's difficult just sitting here talking to you when I've got this raging hard-on."

It was not the most romantic overture, but it served its purpose. I thought about Chuck's admonition.

"You know, I really like you, Greg, and I'd like to get to know you better, without sex getting in the way. I suppose we could just kiss," I offered.

"Why not?" he replied.

Within minutes, our clothes were in a pile next to the sofa.

"I'd like for you—no—I can't say it," he whispered.

"Go on, tell me."

"I want you to punish me, for being a bad boy."

"Maybe we can work up to that," I replied.

Afterward, when we were lying naked on his bed, I opened my eyes and stared up at the ceiling fan, watching it spin in circles. "I'm so glad we waited," I said and then added, "It will mean so much more after we get to know one another."

He chuckled, sat up, and said, "I hope you don't mind, but I've got a dinner with some friends. It's their anniversary, so…"

"No, of course," I said. I hopped up from the bed, walked into the living room, and stooped down, separating my pile of clothes from his. By the time I was dressed, through the sliver of the open bathroom door, I watched Greg wash away any remnants of me. He shouted from the shower that he would call me. I slipped through the back door. On the drive home, my mind filled with the image of a washing machine agitator bobbing up and down, sloshing and immersing the pile of his dirty clothes and sheets down into the soapy water, removing the stains and transforming the fabric.

A few weeks later, in my frenzy to fill the hole of time left by the missing texts and emails from Greg and the unanswered telephone messages I had left for my daughters, I spread myself as thin as possible and went out on dates with many men within my ten-mile-radius dating pool, which was drying up and exposing men like Scott.

"I just adore your Southern accent," Scott said. His elbows were now perched on the table, and he rested his chin on a little platform he had created by placing one hand on top of the other.

"Oh, is it that obvious?" I asked.

"Oh, honey, you are too cute. 'Is it that obvious?'" he replied.

"You have a different accent," I said. "I can't quite place it."

But I could. It was from the 1940s. He'd lifted it from a Hollywood starlet.

"Milton," he replied smiling, tilting his head, but not moving from his perch. "Just a hop, skip, and a jump down the road."

I wanted to skip out of this date, but I stayed glued to my chair. I could not bring myself to say I had some phantom anniversary party for friends to attend. *A Southern Gentleman*, I thought. I should have picked a different tagline for my profile.

"Well," Scott said, shaking his head a little before looking down, smoothing the wrinkles from his napkin. "It's clear that we have a connection. I'd love to see you again."

"That would be great," I lied.

When dinner ended, he insisted on walking me to my car, hooking his arm through mine as we walked on the sidewalk along Moody Street in Waltham Center. I glanced nervously about the street for people who might be whispering or pointing at us. When we reached my car, he pulled a package of breath mints from his pocket, popped one in his mouth, and rested his hand on my waist.

"Mint?" he offered.

I was in danger of becoming a human French fry. I did not mask my horror.

"Scott, I just want you to know that I think I'm becoming serious with another guy."

I could not be Scott's leading man, but he could not see it. Just as I could not become the obedient and attentive dog that Ray had wanted or the gay father that Greg was in need of, though I tried. Like the junked-up washing machines Greg collected, we were all broken in some way, hoping to be restored by someone who had the missing pieces. If there was an owner's manual to my heart, I needed to take the time to study it before allowing anyone else to tinker with me. I *was* becoming serious about another guy. I just did not know who he was yet. But, I knew who he wasn't.

"Well," he huffed. "You might have told me that before I got all gussied up."

I watched him storm away as the end of our date crashed in a terrific fireball. Was I just horrible?

Divorce and Evolution: A Case Study of a "Joto"

Andrew L. Huerta

"You're a deeply unhappy man." Those were the words of my ex-wife. Words she used to describe me before filing for divorce. She said them to me as we sat together at a restaurant, where I was trying to convince her not to give up on me, not to change our lives and leave me alone to face the truth about myself and my future. But she had already begun to change her life.

While she was still married to me, she ran off one evening with her receptionist at work. Not an exotic character by any means or even a typical cliché in the story of a philandering wife. Her receptionist at work was a man, but he was no Greek god. If anything, he was the exact opposite. He was younger than her by two or three years, less educated than her—having dropped out of college right before completing his bachelor's degree—and terribly out of shape. A twenty-eight-year-old with an extended, bloated beer belly and male pattern baldness. He was an awful receptionist too. He could not spell and scribbled cryptic, illegible messages on the old-fashioned pink message pads at her work. And he consistently exuded the pungent smell of body odor due to the fact that he had to walk everywhere in our small town because of his several DUIs. Even a few of his coworkers called him stinky to his face. All in good fun, of course, because what they said behind his back was much worse. So at the end of our marriage, my ex-wife had become a huge joke that everyone I knew was laughing at.

At the time of my divorce, I was thirty years old. My ex-wife had completed her education and established a successful career, while I was still working on mine. As a wannabe writer, I had just completed my master's degree in English and was working in human resources at our small-town university, my alma mater. I drank too much, I worked too little, and I was angry all the time. My ex-wife was absolutely correct. I was deeply unhappy.

In retrospect, I would describe my twenties as a decade of fear. I was deathly afraid of anyone finding out that I was gay, so I decided to marry a woman to help me remain in the closet. I needed to try to convince myself that I was not gay and that I could fulfill what I perceived to be everyone's expectations of me. To be the smart young man who could have it all: exemplary marriage, intelligent wife, beautiful children, immaculate house, and successful career. I knew at the time that I was forcing a circular peg into a triangular hole, but there was just no stopping me.

At this point in my life, I have been reflecting on three questions concerning my past in order to assist others in understanding why some gay men marry women. Especially gay men of Generation X and what some of us faced as closeted young men.

The first question is one that I am asked most frequently: If you knew you were gay, why did you marry a woman? But even before addressing that, I have to consider what placed such a high level of fear into me during my formative years and address the question: Why did you stay in the closet for so long? I also believe that it is important to answer for as many people as possible one final question: What did you do to change the persona you had developed as a deeply unhappy man? In working through these questions, I hope to share my experience as a case study of a gay man, or "joto," who lived with an affected straight identity for so long. I wish to show support to other gay men of any generation who might be working their way out of the closet and dealing with such issues as family expectations and irrational levels of fear.

The Gay Examples in My Family

I was afraid of everything when I was younger, and I was terrified of letting people get too close to me. If they got too close, they could possibly get to know the real me, and that would be unsafe. I was called gay or fag or joto all the time by bullies at school, friends, and family members, and I never wanted people to realize that what they were saying about me was true. That I was gay. That I wanted to be with men. That I would be happy finding a husband and living a traditional married life with a man, not a woman. So when I was younger, I hid as much as I could, even as I lived in the middle of a large ambitious family or shined as the star student or star athlete. I was shy. I never talked more than I absolutely had to, and I was a loner who kept his distance from everyone. These days others would just label me as an introvert. An introvert who is more interested in his own world than sharing his true identity with others. But then again, living as a young person in these days of information overload and media saturation, I would hopefully have a more realistic understanding of what my life would be like outside of the closest.

One of my earliest fears developed from a story I had heard, essentially an old gay urban myth that made me afraid of other men in public restrooms. I'm not quite sure who first told me the story, but I remember other boys recounting it in my first-grade classroom. The story consisted of a young boy (always the age of the boy you were telling the story to) who went into a public men's room by himself. Seems the boy was looking at other men's penises while taking his pee, and a few young men in the bathroom yelled at him, told him that what he was doing was wrong. And then one man held him down while the other took out a knife and cut off the boy's penis. Balls and all. These are the stories that young boys shared in my first-grade classroom, and they served as a warning of what not to do, or how not to behave, when you are around other men in a public restroom. To this day I don't think I ever enter a public restroom without thinking about this gay urban myth.

My other fears of letting people know that I was gay came from family members. Family members who, as examples of gay men, taught me of the many dangers that one could encounter living a life outside of the closest. When I was ten years old, I attended the funeral of my first cousin, who we called Little Louie. This funeral is memorable due to the fact that Little Louie was the first of the grandchildren in my family to die, and that this funeral had a bit of flair to it. While it was a typical Catholic funeral, with the full Mass, a eulogy instead of a homily, and the offering of holy communion (the body of Christ in the form of a little circular wafer), one of the altar boys had been enlisted to provide an odd performance next to my cousin's casket. The altar boy, who must have been thirteen years old, held out in front of him, in various positions in the air, a long metal sword that looked like something out of a King Arthur movie. As the mass progressed, probably every three or four minutes, the altar boy would strike a different pose and display the sword dramatically in front of him: up in front of his face, then up and out to his left side, then over and out to his right side, but never pointed down toward the ground. And the altar boy was really into it. He had a serious expression with each and every pose. He never cracked a smile or broke character. I have never since seen a sword-wielding altar boy provide such a performance next to a casket at a funeral.

While the altar boy was just an added reminder that my cousin was different and had a flair for the dramatic, it's the story of Little Louie that always served as a warning to me of the dangers that lie outside of the closet for gay men. Little Louie was of course gay, and while he never officially came out of the closet, everyone knew he was gay. They knew because he was one of the best hairdressers in town (he had bleached his jet-black hair a dramatic blond and had it teased up high on top of his head) and he moved to San Francisco to live life on his own terms. A few years after establishing himself in San Francisco as a successful hairdresser, Little Louie was killed in a dark alley one night by several men with baseball bats. They literally beat him to death because of who he was or who they saw in his physical appearance. No one at the time ever referred to his death as the result of gay bashing. If anything, it was said that what happened to him was a result of how he carried himself. It was something that just happened to men like him. Those are the comments, and this is a story that leaves an impression on a young person's mind. Even at the age of ten, I remember being terrified of the threat of physical violence that went along with being gay. The idea that I could eventually become a victim of violence scared the hell out of me, and I knew that I had to hide the fact that I, too, was one of those men, a man just like Little Louie.

While Little Louie serves as one of the earliest examples of a gay man in my family, the second example is a cousin I knew a bit better. My cousin Joe was an incredibly handsome young man. He married a beautiful woman when he was young, they had a dog that I just loved named Galadriel, and he always talked of becoming a veterinarian. When I was younger, I thought my cousin Joe was amazing, and I adored him and his wife. But as time progressed, everyone began to talk about how unhappy Joe had become. He divorced his wife, began to drink a lot, too much actually, and began using drugs. I never really knew the details of his drug abuse until one day he sent some photographs to my older brother. My brother told me that Joe had taken a turn for the worse and showed me a few of the photographs. They were of Joe in nothing but thong underwear with a crack pipe in his hand. My brother said it was Joe's way of coming out, both as a drug addict and a homosexual. To me, the two went hand in hand. At the time I was twenty years old. I remember staring at one photograph and feeling an incredible sadness. I knew my young, smart, handsome cousin had been suppressing his homosexuality through drug abuse. That he had been beating himself up for who he was, physically punishing himself for being gay, and he couldn't take it anymore. His years of radical behavior began to make sense. And all of this again perpetuated my fear of who I was, and it made me contemplate what I would possibly do to myself to hide my true identity.

Within the next two years, Joe was in and out of rehab, got himself a boyfriend who everyone in the family referred to as "Miss Thang," and lived his life as best he could. He eventually lost most of his eyesight due to his drug abuse, moved in with and became totally dependent upon his mother, and died before he reached the age of fifty. Joe was again an example in my family of what life does to a gay man.

But the most prevalent example of a gay man in my family was Uncle Joe, who I consistently experienced a love/hate relationship with. While Uncle Joe was generous, and I knew that he loved me in his own way, to me he often revealed a side of himself that was extremely sarcastic and bitter. I was a teenager when I spent the most time with him, and to me he was like one of those gay stereotypes you see in old movies like Mart Crowley's *The Boys in the Band*. He was a bitter old queen who liked to have fun but never quite knew where to draw the line between what was funny and what was hurtful, sarcastic, or demeaning. I often think that my uncle saw himself in me. That I was just this young gay teenager who didn't know what life held in store for him. And he didn't quite know how to treat another gay Huerta boy following in his footsteps. Being a mentor or even a confidant was something that was way beyond his comprehension.

While my uncle lived a good life, with a long-term relationship with his partner, great success in the family restaurant that kept many members of the family afloat financially, consistent travel throughout Mexico, and a series of large luxurious houses, there was always something about his disposition that kept me at a distance. At the age of thirteen, I went to work at the family restaurant, a large Mexican restaurant on the west side of Tucson. As an impressionable young man, I began to take in the details of who my uncle really was. My uncle would often show up at the restaurant in his short white tennis shorts and carry his vinyl bank bag under his left arm like a clutch purse. Most of his necessities were in his Valley National Bank bag, and I believe the makeshift clutch might have also held a few things to do with the bills or payroll at the restaurant. But I only saw him pull his car keys, cash, or a small compact mirror out of his clutch purse.

Uncle Joe died when I was twenty-two years old. At the time I was away at college, finishing up my undergraduate degree. I remember sitting in my dorm room feeling angry. I was angry at the fact that all I knew of him was his sarcasm and what I perceived to be his cold-heartedness. To most everyone else he encountered, Uncle Joe was a friendly man, but to me, he was a sarcastic old queen. That was the gay stereotype that I might have been related to but never wanted to live.

As examples, these men were all I knew of the lives of gay men. They may not have come out of the closet officially, made their announcements to the entire family, but they never hid who they were, and they didn't live their lives on the down low. But each one of them, as well as several other closeted examples in my family, taught me about who I am or who I could potentially be. And all three of these men helped in establishing my fears. Fears that were molded by the threat of physical violence and then set by the idea of developing an identity based on self-loathing, sarcasm, and bitterness.

The Straight Examples in My Family

While I have learned a great deal from my family about who not to be, my parents, at the other end of the spectrum, serve as an example of a strong couple who fell in love at a young age and have persevered through over sixty years of marriage. My father met my mother at a high school dance. They each came to the dance with their own dates but left together. In high school, my dad was the big man on campus, even though he was five feet five inches tall and weighed about 125 pounds. Everyone knew my father, and he is the type of man who attracts attention without ever having to say a word. My father is charismatic and empathetic. There is not much he cannot do, and if anyone is lost or in need of assistance, my father is the type of man you can approach without any fear. My father's just a little guy, but the man can get stuff done, and he exudes a positive energy.

What first attracted my mother to my father was that he was a good dancer. And my mother, who was about the exact same size as my dad in high school, was an excellent dancer. Seems they danced the night away after they found each other and have been together ever since. At the time, my mother was the new girl in town. She had been born and raised in West Bridgewater, Massachusetts, and moved to the dry desert of Tucson because of my grandfather's asthma. My mother was also the pretty gringa, looking like a nice mixture between the younger versions of Judy Garland (more *Babes on Broadway* than *The Wizard of OZ*) and Shirley Jones (more *Carousel* than *Oklahoma!*), and she was inquisitive and assertive. All of this attracted my father right away. After dating for a short time and poorly utilizing their first method of birth control, which was prayer, they married twice in two separate ceremonies: a rushed wedding at the courthouse and a larger wedding with all of the family.

Since then my parents have been seen as an exemplary couple that everyone compliments. I have friends from high school who still talk about how cute my parents are. And my friends also say that my parents give them hope, especially when it comes to longevity in the wonderful institution of marriage. As the exemplary couple, my parents have set the stage for other successful marriages in my immediate family. I have seen my sister Monica find the love of her life and marry him in a ceremony that was very much like the one Julia Roberts has in *Steel Magnolias*. My sister Adrian is also in a happy marriage that has lasted twenty-five years, and my sister Leehla found her true soul mate in her partner, Wendy. Good marriages tend to be standard in the Huerta family, and when I met my ex-wife, who was everything I thought I was looking for, I knew I had found someone I could marry.

The plain truth about my marriage is that I fell in love. At the time I saw my ex-wife as smart and pretty, and she and I shared the exact same background. I could not have found a better match. My ex-wife is half Latino like me, with her white father and Mexican-American mother; was raised Catholic; had parents who were still together after twenty years of marriage; and was so ambitious that I knew we could help each other earn our advanced degrees and move into impactful careers. We thought alike, we loved to have a good time, and we became a couple very much like the examples I had come to know. Here I was, a man totally confused about his sexuality, and I had found the ideal mate to marry and start a family with.

At the time of my marriage, all I really knew was that I wanted to become a father. In my extended family, most everyone has at least three children. I have a ton of first cousins who went on to marry and provide me with a ton of second cousins. In my midtwenties, children were everywhere, and I wanted to have my own added to the brood. But with the two of us continuing our educations, we found that by the time we had completed our advanced degrees, we had changed so much. My work during my master's program had really opened up the right side of my brain. So much so that I began to fully explore who I was and who I wanted to be. I was writing dark stories about men who were alcoholics and searching for something that they just couldn't find or couldn't come to grips with. My stories brought about my unhappiness, and my unhappiness brought about my anger. I would easily fly off the handle with any small argument, or experience a long crying fit that I couldn't justify. Instead of seeking counseling or working through the problems we were having as a couple, my ex-wife found comfort in the arms of her receptionist at work. It was a betrayal that went beyond our life together and involved everyone in my family. Not only had she cheated on me, she had cheated on a family that had helped support her and make her into the successful young woman she had become. The betrayal added to my anger, but thankfully I began to see it for what it really was. It was my chance out. Out of a marriage that I thought I'd wanted but really didn't. Out of a life that I had been raised to live but never wanted. And eventually it led me out of the closet as I was able to admit to myself and the rest of the world that I was gay. What I wanted was to find a man who could love and support me the way my mother and father love and support one another, to live a life like the exemplary relationship I had been exposed to all of my life. I had tried it the traditional way, a marriage between a man and a woman, and it had failed. Now I wanted to try it a different way. A way where I could find some happiness and move beyond the deeply unhappy man I had become.

The Changing of the Persona

After my divorce, my life went on hold for about a year. I was alone, living about four hours away from my parents and my best friends, but I was able to make a life for myself staying in our old apartment and remaining in my position in human resources. Although I spent most of the year applying for jobs back in Tucson, I came to know the great people I worked with. People who rallied around me to provide the friendship and support I needed. I came to appreciate my new friends, and I learned to appreciate my independence. At this time I decided to really get to know my parents. I spent a lot of time listening to their stories and understanding what made them such a strong couple. What I learned from my parents is that no matter how hard you work at your job or at maintaining your quality of life, you also have to work hard at being happy. You need to put forth effort, you need to focus on your happiness, and you need to listen to your life. My life was now taking me in many different directions, with traveling, spending more time with family and friends, and working in education and impacting the lives of young students. But my life was also telling me that I was alone and that I needed to find someone to share these new elements with.

One night at dinner with some friends, I asked my friend to read me my horoscope. She was looking at movie times in the *Tucson Weekly*. My horoscope told me to be brave, take a chance, and I would find the person I was looking for. Well, with a bit of bravery, I left my friends and headed to the local gay bar. They went to go see their movie, and I went to the bar by myself. For me, walking into a gay bar by myself is terrifying. But I put on my fake, brave face, made my way into the bar, and began playing trivia with all of the other gay men. After a few drinks, I loosened up a bit. Soon the cutest guy at the bar was sitting next to me. I have now been sitting next to that cute guy for the past twelve years. That night has now become a classic Tucson gay story about the one-night stand that turned into a long-term relationship. It's the story of how Dan met Andrew—only now everyone calls us Dandrew.

These days few people even know that I was once married to a woman. And often it seems as if I am coming out of the closet again when I admit that I am a man who previously experimented with heterosexuality and had a starter marriage. People often ask me if I have any regrets, and I always admit that I do. I regret the fact that I got married to a woman when I was younger, even though I know it taught me everything I needed to know in order to live my life as an open and proud gay man. But I say that I regret getting married due to the guilt that I now feel. Guilt that is often hard to explain to myself and to the others who ask me about my past. I know that as a younger person, I was weak and did not have the strength that I now experience every day. I did not know my limits, and I did not know how to push myself to find my happiness and live my own truth. I remember being attracted to other boys when I was in the first grade. I knew when I was walking down the aisle with my ex-wife that what I was doing was a lie. That I was pretending to be something I was not, because I was so afraid of living my life as a gay man. Afraid of who I was, because I was different, and I did not want to become another tragic story in the history of gay men in the Huerta family.

Fear is a strange thing. And my fear was irrational. I now know that my parents would have accepted me if I had come out to them as a gay man at the age of twenty. I know that I could have lived my life without getting beaten to death by men with baseball bats, or becoming addicted to drugs and eventually losing my eyesight, or possibly becoming a bitter old queen who does not know the difference between being funny and being cuttingly sarcastic. But I also know that my fear was my reality when I was younger, and it has taken me a lifetime to work through that fear and work toward finding and maintaining my happiness.

My Evolution

These days no one knows me as a deeply unhappy man. Today if you were to ask my family, friends, colleagues, or even the one hundred students I work with every year, they would say that they see me as a happy middle-aged man. A man who is serious and stern, but knows how to have a good time, and knows how to find the enjoyment in life.

Since my divorce I have led a somewhat nontraditional life. I returned to school and earned my PhD in education. I took a demotion at work and went from a full-time director to a part-time coordinator to focus on my doctoral work and eventually secure a position as an adjunct faculty member. I have placed my relationship in jeopardy several times by wanting to focus on my writing and not wanting to pursue a more administrative, financially stable career in academia. And through all of this, I have worked hard at maintaining the happiness I have found outside of the closet. I have been able to admit to myself and anyone else who will listen, who I am, what I want out of life, and that I am unfortunately a man who lives with regret. However, I am also a man who listens to his life. I have learned from the mistakes of my past and the mistakes that have been made by others. My evolution is the product of being able to reevaluate my fears and change them into more rational perceptions of my strengths and abilities.

These days I am not afraid to admit who I am, and there are honestly few things that frighten me. My regrets are still present, but they are an accepted part of my past. I am at peace with the fact that I have not been able to have children and feel blessed that I experience incredibly close relationships with many of the students I work with. Through reflection and acceptance, I have been able to bring about my own evolution. I have been able to change my persona to one of a resiliently happy homosexual man. I will never again allow anyone to see me, or even describe me, as a deeply unhappy man.

Lying through Living

David B. Livingstone

For all sad words of tongue or pen,
The saddest are these: "It might have been!"

—John Greenleaf Whittier

I came out after a full half century of existence. Came out publicly as bi, that is, and in about as public a way as a generally anonymous person can manage: via a rather roundabout blog entry, amplified by a Facebook post.

Unlike my typical Facebook posts, which attract about as much attention as old Wayne Newton albums, this one seemed to travel at warp speed through a vast network of did-you-hears, racking up "Likes" and kind, supportive comments—much more attention than I had wanted or intended. This surprised me, as did the fact that so many seemed surprised, including many of the people who had thought they knew me best. Which, when I thought about it, made me a little sad.

I had succeeded in going through most of my life without most people I knew knowing me *that well*. Making it to the half-century mark effectively as, in Alan Watts's words, a "genuine fake." In the days and weeks before this grand pronouncement, I'd begun to take stock of exactly what the payoff of living this way had been, and it hadn't been much—an illusory sense of stability and security, as thin and fragile as a moth's wing, serving as a buffer between a hostile world and an approximation of myself.

It had probably helped me get jobs. It had probably reduced the frequency with which I got my ass kicked, in school or on the street. It had allowed for a fragile peace within my nuclear family, enabling some questions to go unasked and some judgments to go unpassed. It had enabled me to initiate or maintain friendships and relationships, of a limited sort, with people who otherwise may not have been inclined, had they known the Truth.

It allowed for survival, which is not inconsiderable. But it didn't allow for living. By the time I came out, I had known for a long time that the former without the latter didn't amount to all that much.

At the outset, living the lie had been essentially inevitable. Midwestern communities packed with Methodists and Presbyterians and Pentecostals and Catholics at the height of the AIDS panic were not places in which to be yourself if being yourself meant being remotely interested in fucking other guys. I'd seen what became of others like me about whom suspicions had been raised, or who had let too much be known. In the adult world, they were whispered about, shunned, or ignored; in junior high and high school, they were isolated, preyed upon, and effectively destroyed. The small number of kids, male and female, whose non-straight nature was unquestioned were effectively quarantined into a caste of untouchables left to be ignored until some jock felt like kicking the shit out of one of them. I, on the other hand, was merely suspect. I got only some taunting, occasional physical abuse, and general contempt.

This passed, of course. College, larger cities, different circles of friends brought an end to the day-to-day bullshit. But habituated behaviors aren't dislodged so easily. Having worked hard to achieve the anonymity of normalcy, I felt no inclination to let it go. It was easier to go on as I had always done, for day after day and year after year. And so I did, for another three decades, through jobs and friendships and relationships and finally into parenthood.

We are what we repeatedly do, the saying goes. When what you repeatedly do consists of weaving a cloak of illusion around yourself, that is precisely what you tend to become: an illusion. I have had a reputation for being rather remote, private—my own mother describes me as reserved—and this reputation was the by-product of this habit, the compulsive need to control how I am perceived. What began as a survival mechanism, concealment of an orientation and desires that those around me at the time considered unconscionable, extended outward to affect almost everything I said and did. Holding back. Filtering what was said. Allowing convenient misperceptions to go unchallenged. And without thinking about it, making sure that virtually everyone who "knew" me knew someone slightly different than the person who actually existed.

All of this was very unconscious, of course. And it could have gone on forever: it had become easy, a matter of routine. My dealings with other people—friends, family, colleagues, lovers—were typically pleasant, typically satisfactory. At some points I would become vaguely aware of what I was doing, momentarily conscious of the idea that the central kernel of whatever it was that constituted the real me was becoming smaller and dimmer in the rearview mirror, even to myself, but even that was largely painless. Fabrication and maintenance of the outer shell happened on autopilot. But then I had a child.

It wasn't until my daughter was five years old that two things occurred to me: that there was one small person who I absolutely, positively had to be myself with, and that this one small person would learn a large measure of what she would know about life by my example. And I thought about the fact that I had largely lied my way through life when it came to certain aspects of who and what I was, things that mattered. And I didn't want her to live like that.

It was one thing to compromise my own potential, limit my own opportunities and horizons, narrow my own range of possible experiences, mitigate my own capacity for joy. It would be quite another to lead her to do the same thing to herself. The first is a forgivable human mistake. The second would be a crime against my own child.

So I wrote a blog post, and an entry on Facebook. Came clean. Received a lot of support, a lot of affection, a lot of acceptance, virtually all of which probably would have been there if I'd done something similar three decades earlier.

It was a defining moment because I decided it would be: it was the point at which I would attempt to reverse course on decades of bad policy, start being as honest as I could manage about who and what I am, start figuring out what that "I am" actually is at this point, and live fully in accord with it.

After fifty years, it seems a Promethean task to unpeel an onion that has grown so incredibly large, layer packed upon layer upon layer in a seemingly infinite regress to a hollow core of—what? A dimly seen, barely recognized essential self, warped by decades enfolded in and bound by the limitless layers of little daily lies, little impromptu skits in which I acted out the role of "normal."

I do know that I don't have another fifty years to fully undo the damage, to peel the onion. Each layer that's removed requires time, persistence, and energy. All too often, I have no reserves of any of the three. Taking inventory of a lifetime's worth of friendships and relationships leading up to this point, I see a litany of lost opportunities to be fully alive, fully myself, rendered so by words unsaid, thoughts and feelings unexpressed, things held back. However good or great these relationships and moments may have been, there's the knowledge that I could have made most of them greater had I not held something essential back.

In lying my way through life, I know I did as I had been trained, just as millions have done before me. A genuine, living self is a dangerous thing in a consumer society; to be whole, to live without fear or a sense of inculcated inadequacy is to be an outlier and a threat. It is also what it means to be free and alive, which is what I want most for my child. Good examples are needed, and they are few and far between. If even now I can begin to be one, it all will have been worthwhile.

Dissonance

Vinnie Kinsella

STILL DAMP FROM THE SHOWER, I STOOD SILENT BEFORE HIM WEARING nothing but a towel. He faced me from across my tiny bathroom, a mere three feet away, also silent. His outfit matched my own. I scanned his hairy body as he scanned mine. When our eyes met, my heart beat faster. I had something I needed to say to him, but the words stayed locked in my throat. I took a deep breath to calm myself. Anticipation was written on his face. I knew what he was thinking: *Say it! I want to hear you say you love me.* He was well aware of my hang-ups about loving a man like him, an unapologetically gay man who didn't give a fuck about who did or did not approve of him.

He was the kind of gay man who held an opinion about which drag queen should win on *RuPaul's Drag Race* and who would light up at the mere suggestion of watching a Meryl Streep movie. I'd avoided men like him the entire thirty-four years I spent living in the closet. I couldn't risk being seen with them because I didn't want anyone suspecting I was one of them. Even though I was now thirty-six and had been out for over two years, I still found it difficult to be around such men. Chalk it up to internalized homophobia, I guess. But the further I got from the closet, the less threatened I was by the stereotypes such men embodied. I even found myself enjoying their company more than I did the "masc for masc only" guys I pursued when I first started seeking out gay friends. Men like the one standing before me directly challenged my need for acceptance among the most privileged members of society: normative straight white men.

White and male, I could do. Straight, I could not. Normative, I could fake. The more I got to know those who couldn't care less about attaining the acceptance I always sought (or who were well aware they could never attain it anyway), the more I questioned my own need for it. I was growing fond of these outsiders, but to admit my love for one was still a stretch for me. If I told this man I loved him, that meant fully embracing him. It meant I couldn't expect him to rein in his gayness when we were in public. In fact, I would have to become as unapologetically gay as he was, standing up for him when others disdained him for simply being who he was. I wasn't sure I could do that, but I wanted to. I wanted him to know I loved him just as he was, no matter what anyone else thought of him. So I opened my mouth to say those three little words, but they stayed put. He just stood there waiting. I broke the silence between us with an exasperated sigh and then exclaimed, "This is ridiculous!" Those were not the three words he wanted to hear. "I can't believe I'm doing this," I said. "What kind of man says 'I love you' to his own reflection?"

When my friend had suggested that I try this peculiar exercise of professing love to my reflection, I initially dismissed it as feel-good nonsense. It brought to mind those old *Saturday Night Live* sketches in which self-help TV show host Stuart Smalley would declare, "I'm good enough, I'm smart enough, and doggone it, people like me!" To use a pejorative phrase I normally hate, it was the gayest thing I had ever heard of. But I trusted the friend who suggested the exercise. She had held my hand throughout my coming-out process, and I knew she had my best interests in mind. I was also eager to avoid another downward spiral of self-loathing like the one I had recently fallen into—a depressive state brought about by the bitter end to a messy relationship. So I decided to give it a try.

Having failed at my first attempt, I psyched myself up and again opened my mouth to speak.

"I lo—"

The words refused to go any further.

I tried again.

"I lo—"

It was useless. The words had anchored themselves inside of me.

Not wanting to see the disappointment on my reflection's face, I averted my gaze.

"Why can't I do this?"

Was it really impossible for me to love him, this man—this me—I saw in the mirror?

My mind began to wander to a time just prior to my coming out, a time when I'd had nothing but harsh words for him.

I was thirty-three years old and living on my own for the first time in my adult life. Throughout my twenties, I had taken up residence in what is best described as Christian communal living. Not quite a commune but pretty damn close. There would be no less than six people living in the house at any time—and every resident was a zealot for Jesus. Many weeknights were filled with Bible studies, in-home worship services, and prayer meetings. The owners of the house, a couple who'd met and married during the height of the Jesus movement of the sixties and seventies, were always eager to revisit the glory days of their early adult years, when born-again hippies gathered together to speak in tongues and prophesy over one another. They were deliverance ministers (the non-Catholic equivalent of exorcists) in the church we all attended. I never knew when I'd be coming home to the sound of people having demons cast out of them: "You foul spirit! I command you to come out in Jesus' name!" Weird as it was, the house had always been abuzz with activity, and it had suited me well. What better way to ignore my own issues than to busy myself with constant spiritual activity? There's little time to entertain gay thoughts when you're too busy hanging out with Jesus's most dedicated followers.

After moving out of that house and finding myself living alone for the first time, I found the silence almost too much to bear. There was no one around to distract me from my thoughts. When the desire to be with other men overwhelmed me, I couldn't just walk down the hall and join a prayer meeting. Personal time in prayer and Bible study helped a little, but I could only do so much of both. When spiritual distractions weren't enough, I tried nonspiritual ones. TV was no help, as it provided me with attractive men to feel guilty about lusting over. The internet, with its easily accessible guy-on-guy porn, was an even worse distraction. Hanging out with my male friends from church was a setup for frustration, as I would often find myself fighting off the desire to be intimate with them and then later engaging in a guilt-ridden masturbation session once we parted ways.

I would occasionally find solace in the company of my female friends, but even that was troublesome. In the circles I ran in, if an unmarried woman was spending time alone with an unmarried man, questions would be raised as to whether or not they were romantically involved. Too much time together led to suspicions about them being sexually immoral. It felt like a catch-22. I could spend time with women without having to rein in my sexual desires, but spending time with them raised questions I didn't want to answer. I felt damned no matter what I did.

Regardless of how hard I tried to distract myself from thoughts of being with other men, I would find myself losing the battle in some way, be it by giving in and watching gay porn or by setting up (and then promptly deleting) profiles on gay dating sites. The only supposed victory I could claim was that I had never succumbed to the point of actually having sex with another man.

By this time in my life, I was beginning to seriously question why God was refusing to make me straight. I had tried it all: counseling with pastors, subjecting myself to exorcism to cast out the demon of homosexuality, fasting (once for forty days), endlessly studying the Bible, and dragging myself to every church service and conference I could attend. I became so good at being a Christian that I became a leader in my church, promising others the blessings of God I could not rightly guarantee and judging them as insincere in their faith when they wavered in their expectations. I even attempted to counsel other young men in my church struggling to rid themselves of same-sex attractions. I did this under the misguided belief that helping them might help me. But my fervent service couldn't make my feelings go away. And eventually, after paying careful attention to the stories of men who had been held up by church leaders as being delivered from homosexuality, it became apparent that the claims made about them were exaggerated. When pressed, these men would all say the same thing, even those who had married women: their attraction to men never really went away—they just kept it at bay for the sake of their beliefs and their marriages. I saw this as nothing more than an elaborate sham—men being falsely exemplified as cured for the sake of covering up God's inability or refusal to do what they asked of him. Pull back these claims of a cure far enough, and someone would shout, "Pay no attention to the gay man behind the curtain!"

One night, the deafening silence in my apartment got to be too much. The sum total of all my doubts and frustrations was greater than I could handle, and no distraction was strong enough to keep me from thinking about how much I had failed to be the man I wanted to be. So I decided to go out and get a drink.

In five minutes' time, I found myself inside a dive bar across the street from my apartment complex. I had passed it countless times but had never gone in, mostly out of fear that someone from my church would spot me walking in and get me into trouble. I had no qualms about drinking (Jesus and all his followers drank wine, after all), but I had serious qualms about being seen drinking by people who believed consuming alcohol was a sin. The bar was dark and occupied by blue-collar men, the very type of men I found most attractive. I ordered a stout and took a seat on the nearest barstool, turning my back to the patrons who no doubt immediately pegged me as a nonregular. I didn't care if I was invading their space. I wasn't there for them. I was there to get away from my thoughts.

Halfway through my beer, the atmosphere shifted. Mellow music was replaced by dance music. The crowd behind me began to clamor with excitement. I remained focused on my stout, not caring about whatever event was being announced over the speaker system. It wasn't until a pair of long legs in black heels and fishnet stockings stepped right behind my pint glass that I understood what was going on. I looked up to see a young woman in a black bra-and-panty combo dancing on top of the bar before me. I panicked. As a good Christian boy, I would never knowingly go to a strip club!

Feeling my insecurity, the woman moved on to dance before another man down the bar. I felt compelled to run, but I stopped myself. *I should stay. This is what straight guys do. I should try to like it.* I was grasping at straws, and I knew it. Nothing about her turned me on, but the sexual excitement emanating off the men in the room nearly short-circuited my emotions. All around me were men eager for sex. For one brief moment, I envied the young woman. I wanted these men to want me the way they wanted her. The truth of my thoughts sent me running out the door without finishing my drink. On my way out, I swore I felt the judgment of every man in the room follow behind me. *Look at that fag run. Boy did he pick the wrong bar.*

My distraction had only made things worse. Instead of getting away from the gay voices in my head, I had given them a microphone. I needed to silence them. I needed to get drunk.

After a quick trip to the store and back, I was watching TV on my couch with a six-pack of porter in front of me. One episode of *Glee* later, the bottles were empty and I had to pee.

I stumbled into the bathroom, did my business, and then went to wash my hands. That's when I saw him. The sight of his man-loving face filled me with rage. I decided to put him in his place.

"You!" I screamed as I pointed my finger at the mirror. "I hate you! I hate your fucking guts! Why can't you get a grip on yourself? Why can't you stop liking men? It's like you *want* to be gay! Is that what you really want to be, a faggot? Faggot! You should just kill yourself! I. Hate. You!"

For most of my life, I had hated my reflection. I had hated him because he was the one person I could never fully deceive. Through all my years of working to appear straight, of doing everything I could to hide my true nature behind a religious façade, he was the only one I couldn't fool. I would look at him and see nothing but a gay man who knew the truth about me. I hated him because I wanted to be him, but I couldn't be him because he was everything I had been taught to despise. And I absolutely refused to accept that he was me.

Even after I came out, his presence was still bothersome to me. I stopped hating him once I accepted there was nothing wrong about being gay, but I had to unlearn my old thinking patterns before I could grow beyond a mere tolerance of him.

That first year after coming out brought many confrontations to my way of thinking. One thing that growing up among evangelical Christians had instilled in me was ideological certainty, even when that ideology was undermined by fact. So what if biology, chemistry, genetics, geology, physics, anthropology, archaeology, and numerous other fields of study had confirmed the evolution of all species? The evidence meant nothing to me then because it conflicted with the interpretation of Genesis I had been taught. "God said it. I believe it. That settles it" was the mantra I had heard growing up. Or put another way, "Don't waste time challenging me with facts."

Although the certainty of my religious beliefs had been waning for a few years prior to my coming out, it took accepting that I was gay for me to concede that all I knew to be true could be wrong. If I was wrong to believe I could change my orientation, what else was I wrong about? Like the seventeenth-century philosopher René Descartes, I felt like I couldn't trust my own sense of reality. So, like him, I emptied out the full apple basket of my beliefs to examine them one by one and throw away any that were rotten. I took the stance of a skeptic, allowing contrary evidence to challenge my assumptions. It might sound like a purely intellectual pursuit, but it wasn't. Beliefs are often emotionally charged. And when you challenge a charged one, it will put up a fight.

I recall the first time I set foot into an LGBTQ-affirming church. I had been raised to believe such churches weren't true houses of worship, that they were heretical organizations under the sway of the devil. Just walking in the door was an act of defiance for me. I went because I needed to know what it felt like to be around Christians who would fully embrace a gay man. Carrying with me the disapproval I received after telling my church community I was gay, I entered into the service not knowing what to expect. I was surprised by how familiar it was, save the fact that there were obvious gay and trans people in the pews and at the pulpit. The songs they sang were the same ones I'd sung at other services. The verses they read were the same verses. Even the people spoke with the same Christianese I was fluent in. At first, this sameness comforted me. I wondered how anyone could say the members of this church weren't true Christians. But in asking that question, I opened the door for many others. Who got to determine the true definition of *Christian*? How is it that so many churches that worship the same god, a god they claim to be unchanging, can hold such opposing beliefs about him? Someone had to be wrong about God. Or maybe everyone was wrong about him. Or her. Or, for that matter, them.

Having never really questioned my own beliefs so thoroughly before, I had to wonder where my sense of religious assurance had come from in the first place. The answer, of course, was the source of assurance for all evangelicals: the Bible. But if the Bible was a source of assurance, then what about the disconnect I saw in many churches between their beliefs about the role of scripture and the way they went about interpreting scripture? In particular, I wondered about the disconnect I saw between what the Bible said about women and how churches seemed to softball these passages or explain them away. Scriptures repeatedly make it clear that women and leadership don't mix. Yet so many churches I knew of, even the most fundamental ones, put women into positions of leadership. They were often given titles like *director* to avoid calling them pastors and upsetting those who took the anti-women-in-ministry verses seriously, but they always functioned as pastors. It made no sense to me that churches would say they believed our lives should always conform to the teachings of the Bible while they worked to reinterpret the verses they didn't want to fully conform to.

All this questioning came to a head on the day when I said my good-bye to one of the owners of the commune-like house I had lived in. The mother of the house felt the need to confront me about my coming out, warning me of the path of destruction I was headed down. She was attempting to rescue me from the clutches of hell. I knew in her mind she was acting out of love. After all, if you truly believe someone is headed to hell, then the most loving thing you can do is try to stop them. But it didn't feel like love. Especially since the conversation began with her saying, "You know I love you like a mother, but..." What exact words came after the *but* I don't recall. It doesn't matter. The meaning behind them was clear: she couldn't love the part of me I was powerless to change.

"How can you disregard what is so clear in the Bible?" she asked. "It says homosexuality is an abomination. Abomination! That's a strong word."

In that moment, a list of other biblical abominations came to mind, including eating lobster and women wearing men's clothing. I thought about all the many violations of scripture I saw at the church I had attended with her, yet they were ignored because they seemed silly or archaic. Her words were meant to convict me, but instead they repulsed me. What came out of my mouth next likely shocked her. It sure shocked me.

"I'm sorry," I said, "but I have a hard time hearing that coming from a woman who holds leadership in the church, who teaches and counsels men despite the clear biblical opposition to that. There are far more scriptures prohibiting what you do that than the six verses that reference homosexual acts."

"That's not the same, and you know it!" she snapped back. "Those verses about women are from a different time and culture and have been grossly misinterpreted."

"And you can't say the same thing about the few verses about homosexuality?"

"No. I just can't. It's heresy."

With that, the conversation reached a dead end.

After we went our separate ways, I finally understood the trap I had been in. By believing the Bible was always correct, I was forced to take up the never-ending task of explaining away its contradictions (both internally and with the historical record) to preserve my sense of assurance. Doing this meant there was no end to figuring out when the Bible was literal and when it was metaphorical. It would be easier and more logical to accept that the Bible was at least a mix of flawed writing and divinely inspired writing or, even scarier to my fundamentalist thinking, wasn't divine at all. My belief in the certainty of the Bible was the first rotten apple I had to discard.

Other rotten apples soon followed, not all religious. Some were simply bad beliefs that arose from ignorance. One in particular was the belief that gender identity and sexual attraction were inherently connected.

Shortly after coming out, I was asked out for coffee by a man I had been chatting with online. I said yes, knowing little about this man other than the fact that he seemed nice and was interested in me for some reason. I arrived at the coffee shop early and found us a table. When he walked through the door, I noticed something different about him. *He has really wide hips for such a slender man*, I thought. *They almost look like a woman's hips.* When he sat down and we began to talk, other things about him began to catch my attention. *He has no Adam's apple. How could a guy that slender have no visible Adam's apple? And his voice seems slightly feminine, but not in an effeminate way.* It was then that I realized he was a transgender man.

I wanted to ask him a million questions, but I didn't know if they would be appropriate to ask. I was so uneducated about trans people that I feared I would say the wrong thing and offend him. Instead of declaring my ignorance and opening myself up to learn from him, I avoided the topic of him being a trans man altogether. In hindsight, my failure to acknowledge a part of his core identity likely came across as me having a problem with trans people.

Later on, I found myself puzzling over the fact that he was both gay and trans. It was an intersection of identity I had never encountered before. I thought about the few trans people I already knew. Most were students I taught in my job as an adjunct instructor at a local university. From what I had observed, they all seemed to date people of the opposite sex. Based on that small sample set, I had assumed all trans people dated people of the opposite sex. It made sense to me: you become a man, you date a woman; you become a woman, you date a man. My mind didn't know how to process meeting someone outside of the sample set. *If he was once a woman who dated men, that means he was straight before he transitioned, right? But now that he's transitioned, he's gay? Or was he always gay because he was always a man at heart?* It finally clicked that his attraction to men wasn't a part of his gender identity. This was an insightful realization for me. Not just in my understanding of trans people but also in my understanding of myself. As a man who likes men, I often questioned what that said about my gender. Perhaps fueled by the misogynistic insults I'd heard lobbed against gay men growing up—sissy boy, girly man—I had internalized the idea that being gay somehow diminished my manhood. Although I did not subscribe to the belief that women were somehow inferior to men, I had for years buried any feminine qualities about myself for fear that letting them loose would only feed the gayness I was trying to overcome. Finally understanding that sexual attraction exists independent of gender was liberating. I came to see that being attracted to men made me no less of a man, and having feminine qualities made me no more gay.

From that day forward, I would no longer worry if my actions were perceived as either masculine or feminine. I would just be me. It was a corner that my reflection was happy to see me turn as it pushed me one step closer to fully accepting him.

Even with that corner turned, there were still things I saw in my reflection that led me to keep him at arm's length. I didn't like seeing the awakened desire in his eyes after I came out. I had spent years perfecting the image of being the good little church boy, and I wasn't about to throw that away easily. For several months after I came out, sex wasn't on the agenda. Although I had accepted that it wasn't wrong for two men to have sex, I still clung to the idea that they should only be having sex if they were married. I had a long list of sexual action I would not do. Eventually, though, I did indulge my desires.

My first sexual encounter with another man was exhilarating. After dinner and drinks, we made out in his car underneath one of Portland's numerous bridges. I felt like a teenager who had snuck out of his home to avoid getting caught by his parents. After a few minutes of kissing in the front seat, we moved to the backseat and started taking each other's clothes off. Although we didn't go "all the way," as teenage me might have said, we went far enough for me to put to rest any lingering doubts about my sexuality. No woman had ever turned me on like he did.

But as exhilarating as that experience was, it paled in comparison to the first time I actually did go all the way with another man. I'll call him Walt. Walt was a handsome bisexual pastor in an LGBTQ-affirming denomination, and we met while I was on vacation. He told me about his experience coming out, and we talked about how, in his denomination, premarital sex wasn't blanketed as sin, that people were free to live by their own convictions on the matter. I found him to be quite sexy, and as an added bonus, he was a caring man. That night I discovered that empathy works as an aphrodisiac on me. Walt's being a pastor made it easy for me to say yes to going to bed with him (if the pastor does it, it must be okay!). It was a beautiful experience—all I had ever fantasized about. I woke up beside him the next morning with a smile on my face.

After we parted ways—Walt going to church to preach a sermon, me leaving to go back home—my happiness was overtaken by an onslaught of guilt. The guilt was not because I had had sex with another man. Nor was it because I had had sex outside of marriage. No, I felt guilty about my lack of guilt over what I had done. Two years prior, I would have shunned any man in my church who'd done the same. I spent days feeling bad about how bad I didn't feel, though clearly the me in the mirror felt no remorse about it.

Those feelings quickly turned to self-deprecating thoughts. *I bet that guy hated me. I was probably just an easy lay to him. No man could ever really want more than sex from someone like me. I'm such a mess.* When the man texted me to reconnect, I broke into tears. *You mean I'm not so fucked up that he wouldn't want to spend time with me again?*

Untangling the complex web of feelings after that encounter took weeks. Through the process, I began to see how the restrictive sexual mores of my upbringing turned something as beautiful and natural as two people expressing connection to one another through their bodies into something vile and shameful in my mind. As a result, I realized I had been handed a set of convictions about what is right and wrong, but I wasn't really owning them as my own. To be honest, I never really had. I'd just accepted them as the price I needed to pay to secure my sense of belonging among a community of believers.

With that community fading deeper into my past, my religious beliefs were losing their value to me. This was scary at first. My whole closeted identity had been built around my beliefs. I didn't know who I would be without them. But as I grew more comfortable with myself and the values that were truly mine, the less I needed the identity my old beliefs had given me. And the less need I had for that identity, the more repulsed I became by it. In particular, I was repulsed by the things I had done to maintain that identity.

Coming out of the closet is one thing. Overcoming the shame that kept you there is another. But different from both is dealing with the guilt of what being in the closet forced you to do. It's easy to tell a man who just came out that he shouldn't feel guilty because he hid who he was, to remind him that it was a necessary defense against bigotry. It's easy to see him as a victim of a prejudicial culture, but it doesn't erase the fact that he lived a lifestyle of lying and that his lies impacted others. For me, one of the biggest sources of guilt I had to face after coming out was the knowledge that I had done nothing when others in my church left or got kicked out after it came to light that they were gay. It happened several times over the years, and each time, I joined in on the judgment against them in order to keep my own secret hidden. I sided with the oppressor to avoid being oppressed. It still pains me to think that there are people out there, some I called friends, who assume I hate them for being gay.

Staring at the me in the mirror, I realized this was one of the reasons I couldn't bring myself to say I loved him. After all, how could he love me back, knowing I had played a part in hurting so many others?

Despite my hatred for the version of myself I kept behind the glass, I had admired him at times even when I was closeted. He always seemed freer, happier, more at ease with himself than I did. Although I did my best to keep him hidden away, I'd occasionally let him out for a little while just to see what he'd do (though I always kept him on a tight leash). One place where he enjoyed this freedom was in my classroom.

For almost eight years, during most of which I was closeted, I taught editing classes in the publishing program at Portland State University. For a sum total of fours hours a week (two classes at two hours each), I was away from the scrutinizing eyes of my church community. My students didn't care if I was gay, straight, pansexual—whatever! They just cared that I taught them well. When I taught, I felt little need to act the part of a straight man. Who I found attractive was of no consequence in the classroom. It was in these few hours that the me I saw in the mirror would show up. He was funny. He was engaging. He was sometimes a little flamboyant. My students no doubt pegged me as gay, but I was always careful to never say anything that would outright confirm their suspicions.

For many people, going to work means putting on an uncomfortable and restrictive uniform. For me, it meant taking mine off. Driving home from class, I would often feel a sense of sadness when I had to put my straight uniform back on. After coming out, one of my greatest joys was the day I left my classroom and realized I would never have to put my uniform on again.

As I stood there in my towel, looking at the man I had once hated, had sometimes admired, and had now grown to enjoy, I felt resolve to push forward with the exercise I had agreed to do. I took a deep breath and began again.

"I—"

"I love—"

I started to avert my eyes once more but quickly returned my focus.

"I love you."

The words had finally broken free. I had done it!

Now what?

Suddenly, my reflection burst into tears.

I was stunned.

I didn't know how to respond, so I asked, "Why are you crying?"

He didn't need to answer. I knew why.

Almost a full year after I came out, I thought I found my chance at true love when I earnestly began dating an attractive man. Attractive, but completely wrong for me. But I didn't care. My desire to be in any relationship took precedence over my need to be in a healthy one. And the fact that he was so good-looking made up for a lot of his character flaws. From the very start, I knew the me in the mirror didn't approve of our relationship. But I ignored him. I had denied myself a boyfriend for thirty-five years, and I wasn't going to let anyone—not even myself—take the experience of having one away from me.

Had I not ignored the warning signs I saw early on, I would have been spared much heartache. Throughout the time we dated, I never felt like I was the object of this man's affection but rather a source from which he received affection. Mixed signals abounded, such as the time he asked me to be his date to a wedding and I asked if he planned to introduce me as his boyfriend. He had no response. It was clear he wanted me there to play the part of his boyfriend but didn't want to actually cast me in the role permanently. He would often blame his lack of commitment on his financial instability, having been out of steady work for months before I'd even met him. Even when we downgraded our relationship to friendship, this song and dance continued. I should have walked away from him, but in my desire to be loved, I found myself always snapping back to him, hoping he would commit to me fully once he found a good job. Eventually, though, he fell in love with another man two states away and decided to move in with him. His parting gift to me was to expose the most rotten of all my bad beliefs.

Just days before he moved away to be with his new boyfriend, he texted me several naked pictures of himself. I had no idea why he did it. He had already told me he had moved on from me. He had already publically declared his love for this other man. I stared at the pictures, stunned. He knew I wanted him, and he had told me he now belonged to another. So why was he sending me these pictures? He was probably just seeking attention, but to me, it was as if he was saying, "I still want you to love me, but I don't want to have to love you back."

I was so heartbroken over the experience that I slipped into one of the worst states of depression I had ever experienced. For weeks, all the negative events of my life played in my mind: my parents' divorce when I was ten, being separated from my dad and older siblings for the decade that followed, watching helplessly as my mother destroyed her home through hoarding, losing almost all of my friends after I came out. In revisiting my history, I saw a pattern of what felt like abandonment by people who knew me best. The loss of my first boyfriend reinforced that pattern in my mind. He was just another person in a long line of people who'd proved to me that I wasn't worth sticking around for, that at my core I was fundamentally unlovable. I even spoke those words out loud: "Why am I so fundamentally unlovable?"

There are times in life when we say things that illuminate the dark places inside us. This was such a time for me. I realized then that I had always seen my true self—my gay self—as unlovable. I believed that to such a degree that I had spent my whole life trying to be someone lovable in the eyes of others. I had never given anyone else the chance to love the true me—not even myself. It was upon sharing this realization with my friend that she challenged me to express my love to the me in the mirror.

As my reflection continued to cry, I felt his tears streaming down the flesh of my own face.

"I do! I do love you!" I said. "And I'm so sorry for all that I've done to hurt you. I'm sorry for all the times I hated you when I should have been kind to you. I'm sorry for all the times I ignored what you were feeling because it scared me. I'm sorry for all the shitty things I made you do to fit in with people who themselves would never truly love you."

"I forgive you," he choked out. "And I love you too."

As both our tears began to slow, I saw a smile break out on my reflection's face. I noticed in that moment how beautiful his smile was.

I noticed something else about the man before me. He was no longer different from me. Instead, he was me. And I was loved.

Fracturing the Mirror
of Invisibility

Joseph Schreiber

THE EXACT DATES ESCAPE ME NOW, BUT I BELIEVE I WAS THIRTY-EIGHT when all the strained and troubled threads of my life fell into place and I realized that the true way to recognize myself in the world was as a transgender man, not as the girl or woman I had been trying so hard to make peace with from an early age. At this point, some sixteen years have passed since I came out, first to myself, and then to those closest to me. It was the end of one long, painful process of self-discovery and the beginning of a new journey. Although I have never doubted the validity of the decision I made to transition, I did make a serious misjudgment along the way that left me as invisible and alone in the world as a man as I had been in my female form.

I grew up in the 1960s and '70s in a rural area on the edge of a growing city in Western Canada. I was keenly aware at an early age that I was different, that I did not fit in with the other girls around me, but there was absolutely no context for the extreme unease I felt about the boy lurking inside me. This was a time when the terms *sex* and *gender* were assumed to be synonymous. The body was believed to be predictive of gender, but society, not biology, dictated and reinforced appropriate behaviors for boys and girls, women and men. Consequently, gender expression was thought to be mutable to conform to the body, causing some terrible surgical travesties to be committed against infants of indeterminate physical sex.

I was never a tomboy, but in my rural area there were no girls my age, so for the most part I played with my brothers or found ways to occupy myself alone. At school I was a shy and awkward outcast. As I got older, I became increasingly aware that I really did not understand how other girls thought. It seemed as if those who should have been my peers were on another wavelength that I could not tune in to, leading me to wonder if, somewhere along the way, I had missed a critical orientation session or had lacked a role model to teach me how to *be* and *feel* female.

In those days there was no context for me to make sense of this pervasive sense of difference, and I did not want my troubling inadequacy to be exposed. In the mirror I saw a creation that appeared to be female but was a stranger. I worried that others would question my authenticity. But of course no one ever did. I struggled with a deep insecurity that nobody else even suspected. Over time, I developed a strong dislike for other women. I was constantly awkward in their presence and struggled to make friends. Unlike the experience of many other transgender men, I never developed an attraction to women. I liked men.

This attraction to men was a false comfort to my unstable gender identity. It provided a fragile sense of external protection against my ongoing fear that others would discover my true "maleness," yet at the same time, it contributed to my long, convoluted journey to self-understanding by leading me away from the growing queer community of the 1980s. While so many of my female-to-male transgender peers sought tentative space in a lesbian identity as they processed their gender identities, I got married to a man instead.

During the years that I existed as an ostensibly straight woman, I found that my gender insecurity would arise every time I reached a certain level of intellectual engagement, as if I had constructed an internalized glass ceiling. This self-consciousness kept me from pursuing graduate studies or entering law school when I was accepted. Really using my brain meant really being *me*, and I could not imagine holding a female sense of self together in the process. It sounds incredible, but

I truly felt that my gender was something I constructed every day—it never felt natural.

So I made detours into safely "feminine" jobs, such as working in a dress shop and a stint as a receptionist. Finally, despairing that I could ever resolve this persistent feeling of being out of place in my body, I decided to have a child, something I had never planned. What could possibly be more female? And I reasoned that if I had a daughter, I could teach her to be female and, in doing so, learn what I still assumed I had failed to master somewhere along the way.

Our first child was a boy, so we tried again and had a girl. After her birth, it was soon evident to me that there was nothing that I could pass on to her. I felt more hopeless than ever. There had to be something else at play. Having finally run out of explanations for my inability to make sense of my own apparent womanhood, I desperately started to wonder if my sexual orientation had been misconstrued. Could *I* possibly be a lesbian?

That line of reasoning was hardly a marriage builder. My relationship had already been stretched thin. So had my sanity. In my midthirties I experienced a serious mental breakdown that landed me in the hospital. But this devastating process ultimately brought out into the open the gender identity issues I had been fighting to subdue all my life. Questioning sexuality opened the door to an exploration of queer identities and, ultimately, my discovery of female-to-male transsexuals, which I'd suspected existed but had never heard of or seen in the general media like I had their more sensational male-to-female counterparts. What a relief it was to finally understand that my long-standing sense of a male identity was my authentic self and that the body could be modified with hormones and some level of surgeries (if desired) to facilitate a life lived as a man.

At last I knew who I was, and I knew what I had to do. Not that it was an easy solution; my husband and I struggled with the issue until he agreed to let me move on. It was a painful but necessary process. I came out to friends and family as a gay transgender man and began the process of seeking out local resources that were, at that time, few and far between in my hometown. I ended up having to cobble together my own support when my expressed sexual orientation and uncertainty about ultimate surgical intentions, were used to deny my acceptance into the existing gender clinic.

At the time I was seeking to start transition, it was less common—or acceptable—for an individual to be homosexual in their target gender. With respect to surgery, transsexual men were often unable to legally change their gender without full genital surgery. However, for men the options can be extremely expensive and risky, and they entail considerable aesthetic and functional compromises. Chest surgery and hysterectomy are now more commonly recognized as sufficient, but that is an achievement that has been reached only in recent years and can still vary widely from region to region.

At this point, I have been on testosterone for about fifteen years, and it has been over a dozen years since anyone has seen me as anything but male. The critical surgeries that were important for me have been completed, and all of my relevant ID has been changed. To those who do not know otherwise, I am essentially invisible again. While it is great to see someone I know and recognize in the mirror, albeit an ordinary balding man in his midfifties, recent events in my life brought to light just how easy it is to become seriously isolated again post-transition.

When my marriage ended and my medical transition began, I found myself the single parent of two children aged eight and eleven. This made it difficult for me to separate myself from the huge comet tail of a past that follows behind any transgender person coming out in midlife. Some men move, some lose all their friends and family, but I decided to remain in the same house and neighborhood. To facilitate a reality within which my new true self could flourish, I created an oasis by focusing on building a career in a new field where no one knew me.

Over the course of the following twelve years, I would dedicate myself to work and family. As I reached a senior management position in a social service agency, I believed I had it made. I was, in my mind, a success. I loved my job and worked hard. The work was rewarding, gave me refuge from the demands of single parenthood, provided human and social contact against my tendency to isolate, and confirmed my value as a man. But the price I paid was huge. I believed that my career was enough in itself and had not imagined it would end. That is, until a year of toxic stress under an executive director with dementia, and a board ill prepared to deal with the consequences, triggered demons that I thought I had left behind before the start of my transition. The mood disorder I suffered from reappeared as I took on an increasing workload, driving me up into hypomania and eventually into a full-blown manic episode. As a bipolar person without adequate personal or professional support, I was the last to recognize how very ill I had become. I left work in shame, unable to even clearly remember how horribly I may have behaved.

Suddenly I was tragically alone in the world. My few close friends were far away. In a city of over a million, there was no one I could call, no one to turn to. I had stayed in the same house, remained actively engaged in ensuring that the schools my children attended were open and diverse, and experienced no rejection from my family. But to create a whole and consistent space in my daily life in which my true past was unknown, I had guarded my history closely at the workplace. Over time I had constructed walls, mastered the ambiguous answer whenever asked about my life, and even managed to successfully neuter and re-closet myself years after originally coming out. This practice bled into my engagement with the community and eventually came to colour my identity in the world.

My longtime friendships had not survived my transition, and I hadn't wanted to let anyone else close enough to allow for new friendships to develop. After a brief relationship early in transition, I decided that romantic aspirations were best put on hold. My job was highly people focused, and my house was filled with teenagers on the weekends, so I began to believe that I could live indefinitely without friends or the potential of love and physical affection. Over time I had come so close to denying my own personal and sexual identity that I had started to develop an internalized homophobia that threatened to leave me emotionally paralyzed.

Fortunately, I had enough insight and enough insurance that the first thing I did when I realized that returning to my job was not going to be an immediate option was to make an appointment with a therapist, an older lesbian woman experienced in transgender issues. And I started the process of reclaiming my identity. One of the things we explored was my connection to other LGBTQ people.

Midlife can be lonely for many people regardless of gender or sexual orientation. As a gay transgender man, my early experiences within the local LGBTQ community had been less than positive. There was no local support for trans men, and I was really unprepared for what I would encounter once I was living and passing as a man in the world. Gay men easily and readily read me as gay, yet when I naïvely identified myself as trans to another gay man, I would be immediately rejected and redefined as a woman or a lesbian. I quickly learned that transphobia ran deep in the gay community, so I kept quiet. When I encountered gay men, typically in workplace settings, I was blindsided by the misogyny that often surfaced with respect to women and the demeaning cattiness of so many of the conversations that ensued. It was like I had suddenly entered a world that was, despite my growing comfort in my own body, again new and strange to navigate.

Knowing of the rejection that many fellow transgender men had faced when transitioning out of the lesbian community, I was equally reticent to share my history with lesbians. There had been an awkward stage on my journey when I was read as a lesbian as my adoption of masculine dress and the slow transformation of testosterone was altering the way I was perceived in the world, but I moved through that period reminding myself that, as they say, "this too shall pass." On the other side of the equation, I exercised caution. At one job where the need to explain my conflicting documents had necessitated outing myself, I found that I was systematically undermined by a lesbian coworker who was extremely uncomfortable with my identity. Thus my early experiences with gay and lesbian individuals led me to understand that the *T* in LGBTQ was an uneasy alliance and left me feeling alienated from a community to which I theoretically belonged.

Much has changed in recent years. However, many gay men are still resistant to the idea of gender as distinct from sex, confused by the whole notion of being transgender, and especially unsettled by the notion of gay-identified transgender men. Once I began to open myself up, with the support of my therapist, to the full acceptance of my sexuality and my identity, I found that I had to confront the deep-seated fear that I had no place in the LGBTQ community. I wondered if I had the strength to risk coming out to others, to find friends and, perhaps, someday, a lover who would accept me. What I had to understand, first and foremost, is that coming out is an ongoing process. And that it is one over which I have control.

I left my job in June of 2014, seriously manic, and by December I was deeply depressed. I had made some tentative efforts to meet and talk to other transgender people, and I had begun to casually engage with other gay men, but it seemed to do no more than accentuate my loneliness and heighten my need to find community. It was at this time, without a scrap of Christmas spirit in sight, I decided to do something counterintuitive: go to church. It had been a good sixteen years since I had attended a church, but I was aware of several affirming United Churches in the city, and the closest to me seemed to have a particularly welcoming and vibrant LGBTQ ministry. I figured that if I was going to find acceptance anywhere, this might be the answer.

What I found far exceeded my expectations. In the time that I have been active in church, I have come to know many wonderful lesbian, gay, and bisexual individuals as well as a number of transgender men and women. I have discovered through conversations with gay men that much of the coldness and social stratification that I have sensed in the local gay community is not unique to my own particular insecurities or me. I have, in safe spaces, started to speak openly to gay men about my transgender history. When I out myself, others are always surprised and continue to treat me and see me as they did before—the greatest validation I could hope for at this point. I am also making friends with other gay and transgender men who have or are coming out later in life. Together we can share our concerns, laugh at our lack of confidence, and ask the questions we dare not ask others.

My hope for other gay, bi, and trans men who are coming out later in life, whether they are in their late twenties or even decades older, is that they find a community where diversity is accepted. I do sense that there is a generational difference for many of us that will hopefully make it easier for those who question their sexuality and/or gender to do so with greater knowledge and acceptance at an early age. My own children have grown up with completely different views on such matters. And of course they grew up with me as a queer parent.

At the beginning one seems to be coming out all the time—to friends, family, and even therapists. But as I learned, once I had achieved that desired level of invisibility on the other side of the process of transition, it was too easy to isolate myself in plain view. As I move forward, I face the constant balancing act between being seen as a man and accepted as a gay male, and knowing that for deeper friendships and physical intimacy to be possible, I have to be willing to be honest about my differently gendered history. At the same time, I have learned that it is important to respect and maintain my boundaries. I do worry about being alone, but I have come to know that for many other gay men, loneliness is likewise a very real concern. I have to continue to believe in myself. In my philosophical moments, I recognize the value and uniqueness of my life journey, but in my anxious turns, I still encounter moments of deep insecurity about my own validity.

But I suppose that is all part of being human.

Pillow Talk

Wayne Gregory

I SLIP INTO THE WARM BATHWATER AND DRAPE MY ARM OVER THE SIDE of the tub. My glass of iced tea and my cell phone are within reach. The phone rings the familiar Westminster Abbey ringtone. It's Terri, my ex-wife.

"Hey. Whatcha doin'?" I say.

"Soakin' in the bubble bath with my book." Terri's voice is calm.

"Me too."

"I thought you always took showers."

"Yeah, but just wanted to soak tonight."

"Look," Terri says, "I called 'cause I gotta know something. What's the right way to do oral sex?"

"Oh my God," I say. "This is like that scene in that movie with Rock Hudson and Doris Day."

"Which movie?"

"You know, the one where it's split screen and they're both in the tub on the phone."

"*Pillow Talk*," she says with her familiar, easy lilt.

"Except she wasn't asking about oral sex," I say.

"She could have."

We both laugh, and I ponder how far we have come in just two years.

Terri and I had been married for twenty-five years, although the last couple had been years of separation and unraveling. Unhappiness and depression had crept into our relationship and into our individual lives, but we held on to our Christian dogma against divorce, genuinely hoping that there would be some chance of fixing things or, at least, some way to learn to live with the pain and disappointment. The only plan we ever had to end our marriage was *death do us part*, but our best efforts at keeping it together came to a screeching halt with a simple question one late summer afternoon.

I sit on the patio under the shade of the Asian pear trees. The August sun splashes its orange light across the yard. I am expecting Terri back any moment from her weekend trip to California. She comes out from the basement door and walks back to the patio. Her steps are slower than usual, almost hesitant. She sits in the Adirondack chair across from mine and looks away.

"How was the trip?" I say.

She grips the wide arms of the chair and turns slowly toward me. Her voice is deliberate, yet gentle. "Are you gay?" Her face is almost hopeful, as if the answer to years of frustration is finally at hand.

My breath drains out of me all at once, like someone has punched me hard in the stomach. The words I have dreaded to hear. The words I haven't been able to say even to myself. The words I have hoped I can somehow avoid just a little longer until something can change me to normal. Deep down I have known that this might happen one day, and now, here it is. I'm incapacitated by irrational fear. I freeze in the face of her simple, damning words. I have no response, only reaction.

"Why would you ask something like that?" I say.

She tells me she has found the email message and the half-naked picture of myself that I sent through America Online to a man in Portland who calls himself MusclemanPDX.

This isn't happening. This isn't happening. The words rumble over and over through my head. I clutch the arms of the chair and begin to rock back and forth. Everything outside me and inside me spins like a whirlwind, unbalancing my world. I am losing my grip. I'm falling.

Terri stands up. "We *will* get through this."

Her last words hang in the air as she walks away. I want to grab them, to pull them into my head and hold them there. But I know they are an illusion. She means it now, but she's in shock. We will not get through this. I am going to lose her. Lose everything. For almost fifty years I have kept the lie together, only to have it shatter in a moment of hushed summer twilight.

That night, I stand in the doorway of our bedroom. Terri has been in bed since she left me on the patio a few hours before. My whole body aches from the weight of my guilt.

She studies me through red eyes. "I don't know who you are." Her voice is far away. "All those years thinking something was wrong with *me*."

I hang my head, and my face melts like a candle.

"I've never had a relationship with anyone. It's always just random. I never even knew their names most of the time." The words sound foolish and unconvincing, but I want her to know that it isn't because I didn't love her. I've never wanted to find someone else.

She shakes her head. "But you were living a lie all those years."

"I've tried so hard to fight it off, but I can't make it go away. I think I'm demon possessed or something."

She runs her hands through her hair and stares at the ceiling. "I can't talk about this right now. I don't even think I can get out of the bed. My legs won't move. Everything's a blur. We'll have to do this later."

I close my eyes and brace for the worst. "Do you want me to leave?" I say. I think I want her to say no, but I'm caught off guard by the flicker of desire for her to say yes.

"No," she says. "But you can't sleep in here."

Tears drip down my face. I sag against the doorframe to steady my legs. I wish I could wake up, that this would all be just a bad dream. I have tried all my life to spare her this pain, to spare myself this shame.

Terri turns over on her side with her back toward me and turns off the bedside lamp. The light from the hall pushes past me and presses my shadow across her body. She almost disappears in the darkness. I close the door. Stagger through the house. Turn off all the lights. I want the darkness.

I slump into a chair on the patio. The moon slips behind a cloud and the stars are nowhere in sight. I weep into my hands and sob a helpless prayer, "Help me Jesus. Help me." It's pointless. The end has been a long time coming.

My life wasn't supposed to end up this way. I grew up in the 1960s and 1970s in a small south Louisiana town full of religion. I was reared in the Southern Baptist Church and eventually became an ordained Baptist minister at the wise age of twenty. Two years later, after graduating from the mothership of Baptist higher education, Baylor University, I ended up back in my small town as the youth and music minister at a newly formed, interdenominational, "charismatic," evangelical church. It was evangelical because we believed that those who weren't born again were going to hell. It was interdenominational because it was full of people from a diversity of religious traditions—Baptist, Methodist, Catholic, Mormon—and those with no religion at all. It was "charismatic" because it was a church where people raised their hands when they sang, spoke in tongues when they prayed, and anointed with oil to heal the sick. I was filled with the Holy Spirit and led by God. How could I go wrong?

Terri and I met in this church when we were very young, very devout, and very idealistic about serving God. Our first date was to a Christian rock concert by a group called 2nd Chapter of Acts, who was performing in nearby Baton Rouge.

All the way to the concert and back again, we listen to Christian rock music and talk about spiritual things, side by side in the cab of my baby-blue Ford F-150 pickup truck.

I tell her I am called to the ministry.

She tells me she wants to work as a missionary in the inner city.

I tell her that I want to one day have an international family.

She tells me she isn't sure she wants to get married and have kids, but if she does, she wants to adopt kids who don't have a home.

I tell her I want to serve God with my whole heart.

She says she wants to do the same.

By the time the date is over, I know I want to marry her.

"I'll call you," I say when I tell her goodnight at her door. I drive home, praying out loud. "Thank you, Lord. I know she's the one you ordained for me. I'm as sure as I've ever been about anything. Put the same love in her heart for me." I think of the ministry we will do together and the family we will raise. A thrill runs up my body. Now, I am going to be free from this unnatural urge inside me. "Thank you, Lord, for delivering me from those sins of lust that have been tormenting me for so many years. I knew that wasn't the real me. I knew they would go away." Amen.

Within three years of our first date, we stood together at the front of the sanctuary saying our vows and committing our lives together 'til death we did part. We had formed a deep friendship more than a romantic bond, but we never imagined that there was any way to live out our relationship other than in a good Christian marriage. We had come to the point that we couldn't imagine living life without each other.

The next twenty-five years brought a PhD in linguistics for me, a master's in education for her, and six adopted children for both of us—the international family we had dreamed of. After finishing graduate school, I left the ministry and we loaded up the family to move across the country to Oregon, where I hoped a new location and a new job opportunity would give me a chance at a clean slate. Yet my ordeal persisted.

Stuggle. Hiding. Denial. Futile hope. I prayed, but with less conviction that it was going to do any good. Finally, well on my way to middle age, I realized that this "thing" I was fighting against was not something I had or something that had me; it was who I was. And it wasn't going away.

While I realized I was thoroughly and hopelessly gay, I had built my external life around the illusion of heterosexuality. When the façade came crashing down on that August afternoon in our backyard, I went into a functional shock. Dazed. Disconnected. Depressed. But, plodding through the monotony of my life, trying not to reveal that anything was wrong. I felt as if I were standing on the edge of a precipice, staring into a wall of fog, forced to leap into the unknown. I had come out. There was no going back on that. But I didn't know what it meant to come *in* to a full life as a gay man. I was afraid to find out. For the first six months after being outed, Terri tried to hold things together and get me to engage. She finally confronted me about getting help.

We sit across from each other in the wingback chairs of the great room one morning.

"If we're going to make this work, we're going to need help." Terri leans on her knees and pushes her face toward me. "You've got to find a way to accept the fact that you're gay."

The naïve hope that I could always count on in her face, the optimism that glimmered in her eyes, it is all gone. She stares at me like she's scrutinizing a stranger.

"And I've got to find out how to live with someone who's gay. I need to find out if I even can," she says.

But, I don't want to be gay and I don't want to be out. What does being out even mean? My only experiences with anything gay have been the random, clandestine encounters with men over the years that left me engulfed in shame and self-hatred. Being gay has been about hiding, not about revealing who I am. I don't know how to start my whole life over, but I'm sure I don't want to.

Terri made an appointment with a Christian counselor, the first of several we tried. It was the only place we knew to go. For months we went from one counselor to the next, but nothing they said helped. It only seemed to make things worse. Terri was beginning to disconnect herself from me. Each day, she was drifting farther away, wandering in her own direction.

I wished I could muster up the hope and faith to crawl out of the hole I was trapped in, but the weight of shame and fear kept me buried. So I drowned those feeble wishes with more shame. And liquor. Lots of liquor. Jack Daniels. Vodka. Southern Comfort. Being a good Baptist boy, I'd been a teetotaler all my life. I had no experience with alcohol. At first it tasted like fire. I had to wash it down with Coke. But too soon, it started to go down easy. I'd drink more to forget, but I couldn't forget. I couldn't forgive myself. I just felt more ashamed, and the days all seemed to mash together. The thing I'd always been able to most count on was Terri. She listened. She championed me. She understood and shared my dreams. There was a lie between us, but all the good we had together had always sustained me, and I was terrified it would never come back. The emotional rift between us had taken that all away. I wondered if our truth and our nearly twenty-five-year history together would be enough to overcome the lie. I didn't know if I could live without her.

One night, I am drunk out of my mind. Sitting at my computer. Over half a bottle of 100-proof vodka in my empty stomach. Terri taps me on my shoulder. The room is a blur. Her body spins in front of me. My insides push out of me as if my body were coming apart. My gut convulses. I throw up on Terri's little white feet.

The next day, a steel gray morning. Terri leans against the kitchen counter waiting for the coffee maker to finish its gurgles and drips. Her arms crossed on her chest. Her lips tight. She tells me she wants me to move to the basement apartment as soon as our youngest son goes away to college that fall.

"Is this it, then?" My voice sputters like a dying engine. "We're not going to work things out anymore?"

The aroma of dark roast coffee saturates the room as she fills her mug. "I don't know what we're going to do. But you're drinking yourself into a hole and getting more depressed by the day. You've got to at least accept the fact that you're gay or else we can't get anywhere."

"I don't want to be…that way." The words tighten around my tongue and stick in my throat. I stare at the floor.

"You can't even say the word," she says. "The counselors can't help us if you can't be honest about who you are. That's got to be the starting place."

I stand in front of the sliding glass door at the end of the breakfast nook and stare into the dingy gray fog that conceals the valley below us. "I just can't get past the fact that I've hurt you and I can't undo it." My words leak out like a deflated tire. "I just wish things could be right with us."

"I want things to be right, too, but I don't like to see you passed out drunk," she says. "And I don't like to be thrown up on."

"I'm really sorry about that," I say.

"I'm sure you are, but I just need some space right now." She holds the mug tight inside her hands. "I'll always love you. But I'm really angry right now." Her words sound clinical and unemotional.

I don't have the strength or the words to say anything. She is only a few feet away, but looks so distant.

"I've spent all our married lives trying to prop you up," she says. "The more depressed you got, the more I tried to do whatever I could to make you happy. I can't make you happy. I realize that now. No one can make you happy but you." She puts down the mug and folds her arms. "I'm spending too much time and energy worrying about you. I need to worry about me for a change."

Her words dump at my feet. So heavy. So final.

Outside, the fog thickens and smears the day gray.

The next month, I moved downstairs. We went days without talking or seeing each other. Every so often I could hear her light feet on the floors above me. It was better than no sound at all, but it made me lonely still. A few months later, she announced she was moving out altogether.

"We need a separation," she said. "I don't want to live in the same house right now. That's not where this is going to end."

We both knew where it was going to end, but neither one of us could bring ourselves to utter the word *divorce*.

"I just wish there was something I could do to make you forgive me," I said.

"That's not my problem. I can't do anything to help you get rid of your guilt," she said.

Her words hit me ice cold. I couldn't hear a trace of sympathy in her voice.

"I need time to heal and I need you to make restitution," she said.

"What do you mean?"

"You pulled the rug out from under me. My whole life has been wrapped up in yours. And now it's all come apart and I'm left with nothing. I need you to give me the money I need to start over and get on my own two feet. You owe me that much."

I did owe her that, and so much more. I determined I'd give her whatever she needed no matter what it took. It was the right thing to do and I had to do it. I couldn't buy her forgiveness, but maybe the gesture could keep some part of her life open to me being in it.

She moved to the little college town nearby where she'd studied for her master's degree. She had always felt something special about the place, but I suspected it was mostly because the move would take her away from me, from the house, from everything that represented the marriage that was falling apart around us. We took out a second mortgage on our house and bought a fully furnished B&B a couple of blocks from the college. She decided to make a stab at turning it into a profitable business. She quit her teaching job and decided to make a stab at supporting herself. She was gone, and the gulf between us seemed ocean wide.

When she moved out, Terri took a few things to the B&B and left the rest with me. Furniture, art, pots and pans, once artifacts of the present, were now relics of our past. Living alone in the expansive two-story house we'd filled full as a family for nearly fifteen years was like roaming through an empty, after-hours museum.

We eventually overcame our reluctance to even mention the word *divorce* and began to talk about when, not if, it would happen. My life began to fall apart even faster around me. I lost interest and energy in things that had once stimulated me. I moved slower. I cared less about everything. The everyday responsibilities that had once gotten my attention, and sometimes my worry, now seemed irrelevant. I now had only my income to pay the bills, which began to pile up. We put the house on the market to get some financial breathing room. Its value had more than doubled since we'd bought it, but the real estate bubble was beginning to deflate. No one was buying. I got behind in payments. Warning letters began to come—first from the bank, and then from their lawyers. Bankruptcy was a serious possibility. Divorce was inevitable. I had always persevered through whatever challenges came along in my life, believing that somehow I could fix them. I had always been determined and unflagging.

"Once you set your mind on something, you're like a dog with his bone," Mama used to say to me.

"You've got more energy and get more done than anyone I've ever seen," Terri had often reminded me.

Yet, for the first time, I was powerless to control where my life was taking me. I had lost everything I had spent my life trying to hold on to. There was no fight left. I could only watch as my world fell apart. Soon, she insisted we get an official divorce. I met her one day at the lawyer's office to sign the papers.

Terri is cordial, nothing more. Her face seems a bit brighter than it has been as we sat at the desk to go over the papers. She nods at the lawyer's explanations, then signs quickly.

I stare at the pages. Couched in legalese, the words seem cold and indifferent. They begin to blur on the pages as unexpected tears gush down my face. My chest gives way to sobs I can't stop.

The lawyer says nothing.

Terri stays put and doesn't rest her hand on my shoulder the way she would have once done.

It takes a moment to pull myself together, but I wipe my eyes clear and sign the papers.

"I thought you were ready for this," Terri says to me as we stand next to her car outside the office.

I start weeping again. "I thought so too."

I think I see some pity in her eyes at this point, but she lets me cry and offers nothing in response.

"I never dreamed we'd get to this point," I say.

"Neither did I." She folds her arms. "I thought being married was for life. I bought the whole idea. But that stuff we used to believe about marriage? About two becoming one flesh? We had it all wrong."

"What do you mean?" I say.

"It's not just giving up who we are and just melting into each other. Being one doesn't come from two halves. It comes from two wholes. And I'm not whole." She puts her hand on my arm. "Neither are you."

We say goodbye and go our separate ways.

Over the next few weeks we spoke only sporadically. The house where I lived alone seemed even more desolate than before. The marriage was over, but the end of it all was yet to come.

One day as our Japanese magnolia tree begins to unfurl its purple-white blossoms, I'm cleaning out the garage. The large door is open and a fresh breeze disturbs the pile of dirt I'm trying to sweep.

Terri pulls into the driveway then steps into the edge of the garage with a box in her arms.

My pulse begins to race as I see the grim shape of her mouth and the dark sunglasses that hide her eyes.

We stand silent for an awkward moment.

I step forward to take the box out of her arms. "What's this?" I say.

Terri shifts her body ever so slightly. She appears to stand taller. Her feet press against the concrete floor. "I can't keep this anymore," she says.

I set the box down and open the top. "It's all our wedding albums and family pictures."

She takes off her sunglasses and moves toward me. "It reminds me of our marriage. Of you. And, I can't—" She stops short.

"Can't?" I say.

Her face tightens. "I can't have you in my life right now."

The last pieces of what I care most about crumble with her words.

"I have to move on with my life without worrying about you anymore," she says. "My body is sick. I'm not going to survive if I don't take care of me."

I know she's right. My denial of myself all those years has also denied her an authentic life. She vowed at our wedding altar to stay with me through sickness and health, for richer or poorer, 'til death we did part. But she didn't pledge to stay with a lie.

Terri holds out a small box. "I don't want this anymore either."

I take the box and tilt back the top. It's her wedding and engagement rings.

"You always planned to melt them together with mine one day and make a pair of rings for us. Remember?"

"Well, there's no reason for that anymore," she says.

My wet eyes stare at her. She doesn't look angry, just empty.

She turns to leave, then stops at the edge of the garage. "I don't know if this is forever, but it has to be for now. Don't contact me."

My shoulders sink and my head begins to reel. "But when will you be ready to talk to me again?"

She slides on her sunglasses. "I don't have to answer that."

My life, whatever it might become, will be lived without her. There
is no us anymore. It's just me.

I watch her drive away, and the sensation of relief surprises me.
I wonder why I don't feel upset, why I'm not depressed and crying.
Now I understand. The inevitable I have dreaded is over. The tears dry
up. My heart settles down. The sadness and pain I have anticipated
take another route. Something like hope rushes through me as if I have
burst through the surface of a dark pool just as my breath is about to
give out. It is not just the end of our marriage, but the end of any life
together. Single and alone. It is time to start over.

The funny thing about losing everything is that there is nothing more
to lose. And with nothing to lose, I had nothing to fear. While I didn't
have any idea of what being openly gay would mean for me, it was
the only life I had now. I knew I had to leave the place of my past and
transplant to new surroundings. I had a little help from the busted
real estate market when the bank foreclosed on the house. For the first
time in years, I needed a place to live. So I looked forty miles north to
Portland, a city I had fallen in love with since first moving to Oregon
twenty years before. It was a place where I had only secretly explored
a life that I was now on the brink of embracing full on.

Yet even though I had begun to tell work colleagues and other friends
that I was gay, I still resented having to *come out*. It wasn't fair that I had
to go through some odd ritual to explain who I was based simply on
who I wanted to sleep with. Heterosexuals didn't have to do that. Why
should I have to explain myself and bare my personal life to everyone?

Then, one day, I understood.

At the university where I work, a visiting poet is holding a reading
in the community room of the university library. I'm sitting in the back
behind a row of three openly gay, male students. I don't know them,
but I know about them and their popularity campus-wide. In all, there
are about fifty people in attendance, a mix of students and faculty, gay
and straight. Like me, the poet is from Louisiana but relocated to the

West Coast years earlier. In his skin-tight jeans and partially unbuttoned shirt, with a white silk scarf garnishing his neck, he embodies the stereotypical gay artist. His poetry is sharp and funny, made all the more entertaining by his breathy and sonorous cadence. As he reads each poem, the audience responds with laughter and applause.

Sitting tall on the edge of their seats, the bright-faced gay boys in front of me seem mesmerized by the poet's every word and animated movement.

I can only imagine the solidarity they must feel with him and the normality it reinforces in them. I remember back to when I was their age. What might have been different had there been just one openly gay man I could have watched the way these boys watched this poet?

Maybe it wouldn't have mattered, given the time and place of my youth. But, then again, it might have given me a sliver of hope that there was an explanation for those dangerous sensations that were churning inside me. But no one in my world was openly gay back then. The only thing close to gay men were the few flamboyant television personalities like Paul Lynde, Charles Nelson Reilly, and Liberace. No one acknowledged the obvious about them. No one in my world ever used the word *homosexual*. Eccentric, they were called, and it was always said with a tone of reproach. Whatever they were, I knew I didn't want to be like them.

But when I see the gleam in those gay boys' eyes in front of me, I realize right then that coming out is not just about me. It's about the collective power of authenticity that gives everyone the freedom to be normal. The reason I felt abnormal and wrong all those years is because I had a skewed presentation of what normal is. Normality is numeric. Being gay becomes accepted when everyone who is gay lives like it's acceptable. Now I can finally say out loud those three little words that have been so impossible and unthinkable: "I am gay."

From that moment on, I was out with abandon. Things began to change. I had been unhappy in my university job for some time but never felt I could leave. I had a good salary, benefits, a growing retirement. It would be reckless and irresponsible to leave a job like that unless I could move to something equal or better. The trouble was, nothing ever seemed to come along. But what had once seemed impossible or foolhardy now felt necessary.

I quit my job, cashed out my retirement, moved to Portland, and wandered into the gay community. I joined the Portland Gay Men's Chorus, began to make friends, and learned about drag shows, Pride parades, and hookups. I also began to write. I had wanted to be a writer since I was fourteen and watched John-Boy scribe his life in a Big Chief tablet each week on *The Waltons*. Over the years, I had only written in fits and starts, and all of it was self-indulgent, brooding, and smothered in religious platitude. But now the writing poured out of me in a voice that was loud and liberated. The more I wrote, the more I changed. Everything I had never found in religion, despite my monumental efforts, now sprang up in me like April blossoms. Faith. Fearlessness. Persistent joy. What I felt on the inside, I lived on the outside. Someone new was emerging in my skin.

It wasn't happening just to me. Terri was on her own path to healing and self-discovery. She started calling more often, and we talked about the changes that both of us were experiencing. She still felt distant, and there was still a Terri-shaped gap in my life. Yet we shared the realization that it's much easier to find what you want when you live who you are. I was standing on my own feet. And she was standing on hers. The experience we shared of each becoming singular was bringing us back together in a different way. We were becoming best friends again, which is all we both had ever really wanted.

The tub water sloshes when I reach for my glass of iced tea. The ice tinkles as I take a long sip.

Terri is still laughing about Rock and Doris. "So what's your advice on the oral sex thing?" she says.

"Go slow and watch the teeth," I say. "And just ask him what he likes. It's not that hard."

"No. That's not the problem," she says, and we both burst into breath-grabbing laughter.

"Can you believe we're talking about this stuff?" I say after a moment.

"Who'd have thought?" she says. "We've come a long way."

I stare at the irregular yet deliberate pattern of black, white, and gray bath tiles on the wall and think how understated her words are. "But how did we get here?" I say. "This ain't exactly the norm."

"I think I had to believe that you were really out of my life before I could get on my own feet and find out who I was, for a change," she says.

"Too bad we didn't know this back in the day. We could've just been best friends and missed out on all the pain," I say.

"Back in the day, getting married was the only option for a man and woman who were as close as we were," she says.

"And as religious," I say.

Terri's voice sounds gentler, softer. "I don't want to do go through it again, but it got us where we are now, and I'm just thankful to be here."

"Same," I say. "Life's too short, and now that I know how to live it, I don't want to waste any more time on regrets."

The bathwater has cooled, and I am ready to get out. "Yep. Just like Rock and Doris, us two." We both chuckle. "How does that movie end anyway? I don't remember all of it."

"Same way they all did," she says. "Happily ever after."

Coming Out Again
...and Again
...and Again

Robert L. Ramsay

TUESDAY, JANUARY 3, 1984. I LOOK AT MY WATCH AGAIN: SEVENTEEN minutes past the hour. I'm sitting in Pastor Rickson's office at Henderson Highway Seventh-day Adventist Church in Winnipeg, Manitoba. His broad back is turned toward me as he thumps away on the IBM Selectric, finishing a letter that he says is urgent. I'm relieved to know that he doesn't consider his appointment with me urgent, though it sounded pressing enough last evening when he telephoned.

"I've had reports about an ad in the *Winnipeg Free Press*," he said, "something about a gay support group for Adventists. I've been told that you're the one behind it."

"Yes, I paid for an ad on behalf of SDA Kinship."

"We need to talk about this."

"I'm really busy at school these days. Could we meet after church on Sabbath?"

"No. I need to see you now. Can you come to the church tomorrow about five?"

Two weeks previously, I had sent the ad to a number of prairie dailies: *Winnipeg Free Press, Saskatoon StarPhoenix*, and *Calgary Herald*.

SDA KINSHIP—A SUPPORT group for gay Adventists. Write for details.

I was thrilled when I received the first three queries. I replied to each one, enclosed an SDA Kinship brochure, and signed off with my own name and address.

I had learned of SDA Kinship a couple of years previously while watching *Coming Out*, a Sunday-afternoon television show hosted by Chris Vogel, Manitoba's pioneer advocate for gay rights. As the closing credits listed gay faith groups, I leaped out of my chair. Had I read correctly? Did it really say Seventh-day Adventist Kinship? Were there other gay Adventists?

In response to my query, Chris sent me an address in California where I could send in a request for more information about the organization. Soon I was corresponding with several gay Adventists, Gary in Wisconsin being the closest one listed on the contact sheet. As the sun set each Friday evening, ushering in the Sabbath hours, he and I chatted by phone. How wonderful it was to have another Adventist with whom I could discuss my personal desires and hopes to one day have a husband. However, satisfying as our telephone friendship was, I yearned for community closer to home, and in an attempt to find others, I prepared the ad.

As the minutes tick by and Pastor Rickson types, I watch through the window as parents arrive to retrieve their children from the day care in the church basement. I speculate on the fate of the little ones in their brightly colored coats and mittens. Will those who are gay or lesbian find a supportive community within the church when they reach their teen years?

I certainly haven't found any like-minded saints. Serving as organist, I often gaze out at the congregation during the sermon, pleading with God to send someone special my way, someone with whom I can establish a loving Christian home. He doesn't have to be particularly handsome, wealthy, or intelligent. So long as he's breathing, isn't noticeably dysfunctional, and can manage his own shoelaces, I'll give him a tryout. Occasionally my heart warms with a flicker of hope when a thirty-something man walks through the doors at the back of the sanctuary.

"Is that him, Lord?" I silently pray. "Oh God, please let that be him." But within moments the new fellow is joined by a lady friend, often with several kiddies in tow. If by some fluke he happens to be single, chances are that he's an inmate from the prison halfway house operated by an Adventist couple.

While the pastor bends over the Selectric, I question what bent our conversation may take. In an ideal world, he will congratulate me for reaching out to God's queer tribe, a segment of the population The Caring Church has so far neglected. He will offer the church's fellowship room for SDA Kinship gatherings. He will tell me that the Women's Ministry group wants to provide sandwiches and juice for our gatherings. He may pass on the names of those he thinks may be interested in joining us, or he may ask to sit in on our first meeting, offering a prayer and Godspeed in our endeavor.

Finally he draws the page out of the Selectric. He reads his precious epistle. Then he swivels around and draws his chair up to his desk. He is a pleasant-looking man with ginger hair, rosy cheeks, and usually a smile below his graying paintbrush moustache. To my surprise, he lays the letter down in front of me.

"I've prepared a letter for you to read and sign," he says, handing me a pen. The letter is addressed to the church board. There is a place for my signature at the bottom. In between is a paragraph asking the board to remove my name from the membership list because I no longer agree with the Seventh-day Adventist Church's teaching about sexual purity.

"I cannot sign this," I say after reading it through twice. "In my thirty-five years of life, I have never missed attending Sabbath services unless I was deathly ill. As a child I earned ribbons for memorizing the weekly Bible verse, the Twenty-Third Psalm, and the Ten Commandments. Every year I attended camp meeting at Clear Lake with my parents and brothers. In my local church, I taught the early teens' Sabbath school class and I played the piano."

I wait for him to say something, but he just picks up his pen and twirls it between his fingers.

"Pastor Rickson, you've only been in Winnipeg for a couple of years, but I've been organist at this church for more than a decade. Even though I'm dead tired after teaching all week, I haul myself to choir practice on Friday evening. On Sabbath, you see me playing the piano for the children. Then I hurry upstairs to teach an adult Bible class. How can you ask me to sign all of that history away?"

Pastor Rickson lays the pen down and nods. "I appreciate all you do. The board appreciates your hard work, but they understand from your ad that you are in favor of…uh…sexual relations outside of God's approved marriage between a man and a woman. Is the board correct in its supposition?"

"I placed the ad to spread the word about SDA Kinship. Kinship provides a sense of community for people like me. It doesn't recommend any particular lifestyle. Here's one of their newsletters. I can leave it with you, and you'll see that Kinship doesn't advocate anything the board would consider wicked."

"But you know what the Bible says about homosexuality. It's immoral, totally depraved. God does not approve of two men…well, you know what I mean."

"I don't agree. Homosexuality may be outside the norm, but my Bible tells me that God deals pragmatically with human beings. Look at kings like Solomon and David who had hundreds of wives and concubines. God blessed them when they were faithful to him in more important ways. Apparently who you love takes second place in God's eyes to things like having a humble spirit and defending widows and orphans—so I believe he probably doesn't mind if two guys, or two women, get together for companionship so long as they're following him in the important ways. I believe God will bless that kind of relationship."

"I'm sorry to hear you say that," Pastor Rickson says. "This is proving very embarrassing for me and for the church. Local clergy have been calling, concerned about what's going on here: the Anglican bishop, a

Catholic priest, among others. And I've had calls from our own pastors as far away as Saskatchewan and Alberta. The only way to clear up this situation is for you to sign this letter. If you do, the action to remove your name from the membership roll will just be a line item at our next business meeting. I'll see that there's no discussion. That will save everyone from embarrassment."

"I can't sign this."

"I'm sorry. In any case, I must ask for your keys. The board won't permit you to play the organ or teach a Bible class any longer, and they certainly will not allow you to play the piano for the children. As you can appreciate, the parents are concerned about your effect on their little ones."

"You've got to be kidding! I'm in their room for fifteen minutes at most. I play the piano while Beth leads them in singing a few choruses. Besides, I'm a schoolteacher. My record is clean. Touching a child inappropriately is the farthest thing from my mind. The very thought disgusts me."

"I'm glad to hear that. Now, I need your keys."

Reluctantly I remove the keys to the church and the organ from my pocket. As I drop them onto his desk, I remember how proud Mom and Dad were when I was entrusted with them. Those keys testified that their second son had grown up to be a fine, upstanding Seventh-day Adventist.

"I'm sorry about this," Pastor Rickson says, standing to indicate that our meeting is over. "I have to follow the board's direction. The only other thing I'll say is that I hope you'll continue to worship with us—and, if you're set in your thinking, then I hope you'll find a partner and settle down as a couple. That's the best way to live."

That's exactly what I want in life, I think as I walk out of his office, puzzled at the dichotomy between his words of advice and his actions.

I'm barely home when the telephone warbles. It's my younger brother John, who is the assistant administrator for one of the church's nursing homes. "I've just had a very disturbing telephone call," he says.

"What about?"

"About you. Why didn't you tell me you were gay? Why did I have to hear it from Mrs. Adams?"

As I listen to John vent, I realize that my naïve faith in *The Caring Church* has ejected me from my closet. This coming Sabbath every Adventist across Western Canada will be whispering and shaking their heads, conveniently forgetting that many Bible writers classified gossip as a sin.

Sabbath, December 10, 1983. It's one of those dull winter days on the Canadian prairies when the clouds hang low, the temperature rises to just below freezing, and the snow turns to brown sugar mush. I'm struggling to keep my eyes open as I drive home from church. Performing in public, whether playing the organ or leading a Bible discussion, sucks the energy right out of me.

I wouldn't be so weary if I wasn't a perfectionist. I blame myself for that. Always wanting to be a good little boy, I took Dad literally when he said, "If a thing's worth doing, it's worth doing well." Growing up on the family farm, that applied to forking manure out of the calves' stalls, eradicating weeds, or playing an accompaniment for hymn singing in church. I internalized the idea that neither Dad nor God would be satisfied with anything less than a perfect performance.

As I drive up the ramp of the parking garage below my apartment tower in downtown Winnipeg, I'm looking forward to my Sabbath afternoon nap. I'll heat up a can of Campbell's vegetable soup, then shuck my clothes and crawl straight into bed. Two or three hours of blessed oblivion will restore me.

My plans change the moment I unlock my apartment door. The storage room door is open a crack. The mat where I set my snowy winter boots to drain is lying in a far corner of the hallway. Skid marks on the white shag rug show where someone has dragged something heavy across it.

Someone has broken into my apartment while I've been away at church. They've had four solid hours to clear everything out. I dash down the hallway to the living room. Relief! My precious Allen organ is still there. I glance into the bedroom. The portable TV is still on its shelf opposite my bed. Loose change spangles the top of the bureau.

Back to the door, I check the latch and deadbolt. They don't appear to have been tampered with, and I'm sure both needed unlocking when I came in. No thief would take the time to relock the door. I turn to the storage room. When I'd left for church, it had been stuffed with several pieces of Brent's furniture and cardboard boxes crammed with his belongings. Now everything is gone. While I've been at church, he and Shawn must have come by to get the last of Brent's things.

I met Brent last July in Victoria, British Columbia. I had rented a furnished apartment in the City of Gardens for six weeks of my summer vacation. I spent the mornings working out at the gym and touring the museums and art galleries. Afternoons I packed my towel and a book and wandered through Beacon Hill Park, ending up on the beach below the cliffs along Dallas Road. The beach was rocky, uncomfortable to sit or lie upon, but it was littered with feral logs, battered and washed ashore by winter storms. Bleached silver by the salt spray and summer sun, they had morphed into natural sun beds.

One day I descended the stairway to find my favorite log occupied. It was a giant cedar with a concave depression on top, perfect for spreading out a towel and cradling my workout-weary body as I soaked up the afternoon rays. That day a blond fellow, about my own age, was lying atop it. "You know you're trespassing," I said, pausing beside him.

"No, I'm not. This is a public beach."

"True, but that's my log."

"Tough! You'll have to find another one."

"That won't be easy. The others aren't as comfortable. Besides, can't you see my initials?" I pointed to where I'd used a broken clamshell to carve "RLR" into the silvery wood.

"Too bad. I claim squatter's rights."

"Guess I'll have to find another one then. You have a good afternoon." I laughed and started away.

"No. Wait up. I wouldn't want you to commit suicide by flinging yourself off the rocks. Come back. There's room for both of us."

I discovered that Brent was also a teacher, working in British Columbia's interior. He had driven down to the coast for the summer, staying with his folks who lived a short walk from the beach. That first afternoon we discovered that we liked many of the same things—reading biographies, hiking, swimming, and cycling—and that we shared a minority affectional orientation. We began hanging out together, and within days he had moved into my tiny furnished bachelor apartment.

At summer's end we boarded the ferry and sailed back to the mainland, where our routes diverged: Brent turning north, me heading east for the two-day drive back to Winnipeg. I expected our friendship would evaporate like the morning mist threading the mountain valleys, so I was surprised when Brent kept up the correspondence. He came to visit me in Winnipeg at Thanksgiving. Still, I was unprepared for his telephoned proposal that he resign his teaching position in British Columbia and move to Winnipeg to be with me.

How should I respond? Physically I found him hot: an inch or two shorter than my six feet two, his body tight and muscular from hiking and cycling. He was gainfully employed, unlike some of my gay acquaintances who drifted through life rudderless. He had his driver's license, had a car—a standard shift, no less.

He was on reasonably good terms with his grandmother, his mother and stepfather, his brother and half sister. He lived a healthy lifestyle, didn't smoke or drink, except for a glass of wine before dinner. In other words, he pretty much met my criteria for husband material.

On the downside, I had noticed during the summer when visiting his friends that he became loud, obnoxiously assertive, and opinionated. I didn't like it when he labeled those who disagreed with him as stupid or deficient in some way. I wondered if I'd have to keep my opinions to myself to preserve the family peace.

However, my devotion to my religion raised the brightest warning flags. Brent claimed to be a Christian, but he didn't attend church or give thanks to God before meals. He showed me the Bible his grandmother had given him. I noted that the gold-edged pages weren't ragged from use.

Sunday meant nothing to him in the way of being a religious obligation, and Saturday, my Sabbath, was his chore day. Would we be able to coexist amiably, or as Ellen White, one of the Adventist Church's oft-quoted founders wrote, would I be establishing "a home where the shadows are never lifted" by hitching myself to someone who did not share my most cherished beliefs?

I had my brother Jim's example. Released from parental control, he had turned his back on the Adventist fold, taken up smoking, drinking, high-performance cars, and women who weren't too picky about whom they performed with. Eventually he eloped with Darlene, who knew little of his background. As often happens, after a few setbacks in life, Jim decided to play the prodigal son, to return to the faith of his youth. Not surprisingly, Darlene resisted. According to Jim, war erupted in their home every Friday night. Hostilities only ceased when the sun slipped below the western horizon on Saturday evening. I didn't want a home like that.

I expressed my misgivings to Brent. He assured me that all would be well. Finally, against my better judgment, I agreed to throw my lot in with him. At Christmas I flew west, spent the holiday with him and his family in Victoria, then helped him load the U-Haul and drive across the frozen prairie to Manitoba.

I told my parents and brothers that Brent was a chum I had met in Victoria who wanted to escape the isolation of British Columbia's interior. He was going to move in with me until he could find a teaching job in Winnipeg. Then he would get a place of his own. Despite telling my family this, I hoped that our relationship would be as enduring as Aunt Mary's.

Mary was Dad's sister. She worked for the Seventh-day Adventist Church's treasury department in various cities around North America.

In 1960 she moved to Denver where she met Charlotte, a tall, rangy girl from Wyoming who spoke with the twangy drawl of her cattle rancher parents. Charlotte, or Charlie, as we called her, was as skilled with an ax and a chainsaw as Aunt Mary was with a crochet hook and knitting needles.

My brothers, cousins, and I looked forward to their annual visits to the farm. Sabbath afternoons we'd beg them to take us for a walk down to the river. There we sat on rocks, dangling our feet in the cool water (swimming on the Sabbath would have been sinful), watching for beaver, foxes, and deer. When Aunt Mary and Charlie came across some odd-looking beetle or snake, instead of screaming and running away like Mother would have done, they stopped, scooped it up, commented on its beautiful colors or shape, then gently set it back on the ground.

I hoped that Brent would become my Charlie, that we would be good company for each other, but within days of shoehorning his things into my one-bedroom apartment, I sensed our relationship wasn't going to last. To begin with, his twenty-four-hour presence was a shock to my sense of privacy. I had lived by myself since leaving the farm at age nineteen. I found it oppressive to come home from work to find someone else underfoot.

As the days passed, it became clear that because of my religion, our lifestyles did not mesh. I loved the sacred Sabbath hours when I could lay aside work and secular things. As the sun slipped toward the horizon on Friday evening, I turned off the radio and TV. I dropped an LP of sacred music onto my turntable and spent a quiet evening after dinner preparing the morrow's Bible lesson or practicing my organ music one last time.

For Brent, Friday evening was the time to go out for dinner, then to a movie, or watch one on television. Saturday was to work around the house or take the car for an oil change or wash. He never complained about me running off to church while he stayed home to do chores, but I wished he would accompany me. I didn't expect him to become a Seventh-day Adventist. I hoped his presence beside me would show everyone that I wasn't completely alone, and that it would shut the mouths of the blue-haired ladies who tried to marry me off every time a single female set foot in the sanctuary.

Growing up, I never learned how to discuss differences in a healthy way. My parents never argued in front of us children, and disagreements with extended family members were rare. Father would do anything to keep the peace, which was sometimes difficult. Rather than call his brother-in-law to account when he was rough on borrowed machinery and returned it in need of repairs, Dad would swallow his anger and fix it himself.

Following this pattern, I said nothing to Brent about my frustration. Instead I created space for myself by heading off to work at seven in the morning. In the evening I increased my workout time at the gym so I wouldn't get home until late. Still, the stress put me off my food, and I began to lose precious pounds.

Finally I found the courage to tell Brent that our relationship was not working for me. He took it much better than I expected. It hadn't been a happy time for him either, and within a month he rented an apartment of his own in a nearby building. I was happy again—I had my own space back but still had a man I could hang out with whenever I liked. I would have been satisfied to continue life that way, but Brent began seeing other men, Shawn in particular. When their friendship took a serious turn, I regretted having asked him to leave.

As I gaze at my empty storage closet that held Brent's boxes just a few hours ago, a wave of loneliness overwhelms me. Tears roll down my cheeks, and I groan from the knowledge that I will probably never fit in anywhere. The gay world is too secular for me, and the local Adventist world is bereft of those who share my affectional orientation.

I slam the closet door and rush into my bedroom. I change into jeans and a sweatshirt. I grab my coat and keys and descend to the parking garage.

It takes two hours to drive to the grange city where my parents have built their retirement home. I know they won't be thrilled with the news of my orientation, but the way they treated my wayward brother Jim assures me that they won't disown me. They will weep. They will pray for my desires to transform, but they will keep their door, telephone lines, and arms wide open.

They see me turn into the driveway and come running to the door before I can ring the bell. "What a lovely surprise," Mom says. "Come in out of the cold."

"I know I was just here last weekend," I say, "but I had to come again."

"We're always glad to see you," Dad says, closing the door and reaching for my coat.

"I made a special trip because I need to tell you something," I say, determined to say the H-word before I lose my nerve. "There's something you need to know. I'm—" My voice chokes up, and tears spurt from my eyes.

"What's happened?" Mom asks, leading the way to the basement rec room where I can see they've been reading the *Adventist Review*. "Has something happened at work?"

"No. Work's fine."

"What is it then?"

"Oh, Mom, Dad, now that I'm here, I don't know how to tell you—" I slump down between them on the sofa, staring through my tears at the magazines lying open on the coffee table. "You're going to be so disappointed in me." I'm blubbering like when, as a four-year-old, I climbed a ladder, then looked down and froze with terror. Dad had to climb up to get me.

This time it's Mom who rescues me. "Are you trying to tell us that you're a homosexual?" Mom utters the frightful H-word while putting an arm around my shoulder.

I nod and take the tissue she hands me. "Yes. Yes. That's it. I'm so sorry. And now Brent is moving in with Shawn. I'm going to be completely alone again."

"So Brent *is* a homosexual," Dad says. I nod.

"We wondered about that when he moved in with you," Mom says, "and there were those letters you wrote from Victoria. You mentioned that he was spending the night with you, which seemed odd to us."

"You say he's found someone else now?" Dad asks.

I blow my nose. "He came by while I was at church this morning and took the last of his things. I'm going to be so lonely." I slump over, my head in my hands as the tears flow.

"But surely that's good if he's gone." Mom pats my back. "You'll be able to get your life back in order. I'm sure you don't want to live this way."

"I can't help being this way."

"Are you sure? Your father and I have questioned the way you spend so much time at the gym. That can't be good for you, being around naked men all the time."

"Oh, Mom, if you could see some of those men, their big white bellies sagging over their—well, you know what I mean."

"But they can't all be like that."

"No, but I felt this way before I ever set foot in the gym. Don't you remember that summer at camp meeting when I was five, how I fell in love with Pastor Scotman?"

"I do remember. That was so embarrassing. You stuck to him like a burr and threw a tantrum when he wanted to spend time with his wife."

"Are you this way because of something Dr. Tate did?" Dad asks. "I guess you know how he approached Allan."

"What are you talking about?" Allan is my sidekick cousin. Dr. Tate is an elder in the local church I grew up in. He's an ophthalmologist. He and his wife are childless but take an interest in all the church kids. At one time they offered to pay for my organ lessons.

"Dr. Tate and Lois invited Allan over for dinner one evening. When he got there, Dr. Tate came to the door wearing nothing but a bath towel. He said Lois was away getting her hair done. Then he dropped the towel and reached for Allan."

"That's disgusting! But no, Dr. Tate never touched me."

"That's good," Dad says, laying a hand on my knee. "Maybe you're not so far gone that you can't be cured."

"Dad, you're not hearing me. I'm not asking to be cured. I'm lonely because I can't find a suitable partner."

"But if you loved women, wouldn't it be easier?"

"Dad!"

"Don't you feel anything for women? When I was courting your mother, it felt so good to hold her hand in mine, to feel protective of her. Do you not feel the desire to be protective of some young lady?"

"No, I want a man, someone strong, muscular."

"Maybe your mother's right: going to the gym, seeing naked men has made you this way. Maybe you need to look at naked women, get one of those *Playboy* magazines, tack the centerfolds onto your wall in the bedroom."

"Dad! I can't believe what you're saying. I bet you've never looked at a skin magazine."

"No, I haven't, but then I'm married to your mother. It would be a sin for me to be looking at other women, but in your case God might overlook it."

"There must be some other way," Mom says, giving me a hug before standing up. "Have you asked Pastor Rickson for help?"

"How could he help?"

"I don't know, but pastors are trained as counselors, and you can't be the first person who has had these feelings. If you confide in him, he may be able to help you."

"Have you told anyone at church?" Dad asks, alarm in his voice.

"Certainly not."

"That's good," Mom says. "I don't think there's any need for Jim, or John, or anyone else in the family to know. I'm sure Pastor Rickson can help you change before anyone else finds out. God will provide a way to escape if you're sincere about wanting to change. Now, you must be hungry. How does soup and buns sound?"

"Sounds good to me," Dad says. I nod. Dad glances at his watch. "The Sabbath is over. We'll shovel the walk and driveway while you prepare supper."

I follow Dad outside where we clear away the skiff of snow. As we stomp the snow off our boots, Dad puts his hand on my shoulder and says, "You say you're lonely, son. You may think I don't understand, but I do. Wonderful as it is to be married to your mother, I'm still lonely. Since the fall in Eden, everyone in this world feels alone. That's why we need God. He's the only one can cure our inner loneliness."

"I know that's true in theory, Dad, but I'm only thirty-four years old. If I get to live the full biblical three score and ten years, that means I have to live another thirty-six years alone. I don't think I can go on without a companion."

Sunday evening, November 4, 1979. I'm walking briskly along Winnipeg's dark streets, my collar turned up against a cold north wind that whips leaves out of the gutter and smells like snow. The hiss of steam in the radiators is a welcome sound as I push open the door at Westminster United Church. I hurry upstairs to the balcony. I take a seat that provides a clear view of the organ console. I'm reading through the program when a voice says, "May I sit beside you?"

I look up to see Roger Ferguson standing in the aisle. "Hi, Roger. Yes, please join me."

We had been introduced to each other at a July organ recital. Roger is a surgeon at Winnipeg Children's Hospital. He's midforties, slim, several inches shorter than I am, with curly dark hair starting to turn silver. He wears black-framed glasses that make him look wise and distinguished rather than nerdy. When we met in the summer, both of us had recently ordered instruments from the local organ dealer.

I shove over to make room for him in the pew. We chat about our organs until the recital begins. Then I close my eyes, the better to concentrate on the music. It's while the recitalist is playing

Norman Coke-Jephcott's jaunty *Bishop's Promenade* that I feel a knee nudge mine. I crack open my eyelids and glance at Roger. Am I crowding him? No, there's plenty of space. I open my eyes wider and look straight at him. He winks and grins, then snugs his knee against mine again. I smile, close my eyes, and return the pressure.

Leaving the church, we walk together in the direction of downtown, where Roger lives in an apartment house a couple of blocks from mine. Along the way we detour over the Osborne Street bridge to the A&W. After ordering coffee and hot chocolate, we trade life stories while playing footsie beneath the table.

Roger is a former Baptist, excommunicated following the divorce from his wife after he came to terms with his affectional orientation. He has an aunt who is a Seventh-day Adventist, so I don't need to explain my beliefs to him.

As we part he pats me on the head, says I look handsome with that dusting of snow on my dark-brown hair, and invites me to accompany him on Wednesday evening when he practices at Knox United Church. As I walk the final few blocks home, I cannot believe that I have finally met a man—and in church, just like Dad first met Mom in Winnipeg's Young Street Adventist Church.

It's after midnight when I let myself into my apartment. I have to teach tomorrow, but I'm too wired to sleep. I lie in bed grinning into the darkness, thanking God for finally answering my prayer for a companion.

Roger is not only a Christian but also a doctor. Mom and Dad will love him because doctors are highly regarded in the Adventist world. Besides, Dad began studies to be a surgeon, then had to quit due to lack of money following the 1929 financial collapse. How thrilled he'll be to talk medical issues with my man. As I drift off to sleep, I realize that I have irrevocably come out to myself. I am a homosexual, but that's okay. God is in the process of providing me with a soul mate, so he must approve.

Wednesday evening I accompany Roger to Knox United. He lets me try out the organ. Then I stretch out on a pew in the choir loft, close my eyes, and listen as he practices Bach's *Little Fugue in G Minor*.

As the notes soar out into the vast space above me, I dream of the life we'll have together: the house in River Heights, evenings snugged together on the organ bench, trying out new repertoire, and trips to France to examine the majestic Cavaillé-Coll organs.

Over the next few weeks, we take long walks along Winnipeg's snowy streets and stroll through the art gallery. We sip hot chocolate at the A&W and enjoy dinner at Oliver's. We discuss the pros and cons of gay relationships in light of our studies of the pertinent biblical passages.

Christmas approaches. Together we attend the midnight service at Westminster United, sitting in the same spot where we first met. Afterward we walk through the silent city to the Ichiban Restaurant, where we exchange gifts. Roger gives me a framed photograph he took of the Assiniboine River in flood. I give him a silver-plated pen on which I've had the jeweler engrave, "Care Fully Yours, RLR."

As we pause outside the restaurant, Roger touches my arm and says, "Robert, I think we should just be friends. I'm not sure I'm ready for anything more than that right now."

"I don't understand. Is it something I've said? Something I've done?"

"No, it's not you. I can tell that you want more than friendship, but I'm not ready for that—at least not yet."

We hug and turn our separate ways. I stumble along the icy walk, kicking at dirty clods of snow as I make my way home. I toss the photograph onto the dining room table, then open the doors to my balcony. I look at the frozen ground twenty floors below. It would be so easy to end my misery.

Wednesday, June 30, 1976. I bid good-bye and happy holidays to my teaching colleagues after our year-end dinner at the Beachcomber Restaurant in downtown Winnipeg. I walk to Dominion News to check out the latest issue of Joe Weider's *Muscle Builder* magazine. I've been weight training for more than a year now, struggling to pack muscle onto my skinny frame.

Muscle Builder inspires me. If I work out diligently, I may one day weigh two-hundred-plus pounds and sport twenty-eight-inch thighs like Arnold Schwarzenegger. Close-ups of Arnold's muscular bod inspire other thoughts too, thoughts that lead to *the ugly habit of self-abuse*, as it's termed in some Adventist publications. Still, I don't twig to the thought that admiring Arnold and his Speedo-clad buds while I'm masturbating identifies me as a homosexual.

At twenty-five years of age, I have heard the term. I even checked out the word during my high school years. I was interested enough to cross-reference it in several different encyclopedias. I learned that homosexuals were sick men who could be blackmailed or thrown into jail for doing unspeakable things. I have never met one, but I assume I may have seen some when I ride the bus up North Main. They're among those unfortunates lying drunk and soiled by their own filth in garbage-strewn doorways.

I scan the magazine rack at Dominion News for *Muscle Builder*. My eyes pass over *Playboy* and *Penthouse*, wicked magazines I wouldn't be caught dead buying. Then my eye pauses on something new: *Playgirl*. What can that be about? I recall the half-shredded *Playboy* my brother Jim once smuggled home from school inside his jacket. He called me out to the barn to share his bounty, but one glance was more than I cared to see. "How can you look at those big tits? They're so ugly!"

I ensure the big blonde at the cash register is busy with another customer. I snatch *Playgirl* out of the rack. I flip it open, expecting to see big tits. Spread across the centerfold is a fully naked guy. He has hair on his chest, furry thighs, and a thick, cut cock! My stomach spins inside my belly, generating electrical impulses that set my heart racing and my penis straining against my zipper.

I check to ensure no one else is around. I flip through the glossy pages: more men, naked men, manly men, my kind of men. I slam the magazine shut, drop it back on the rack, grab *Muscle Builder*, head for the cash desk, turn back, grab *Playgirl*, grab *Playboy*, hurry to the desk. The big blonde smiles, points to the thunderheads on the horizon, and advises me to hurry home before the storm hits. I take her advice, clutching the brown paper bag to my side as I dash the three blocks to my apartment.

Once there I prove that I'm not one of those Main Street degenerates by methodically wading through *Playboy*. Some of the articles are interesting, but whenever I come to a photo feature, I shut my eyes. I feel intense embarrassment for these women who are displaying themselves so wickedly. I recall a Bible verse: "Finally, brethren, whatsoever things are true, whatsoever things are honest, whatsoever things are just, whatsoever things are pure, whatsoever things are lovely…think on these things." I slam the magazine shut—these images are anything but lovely.

I stroll into the kitchen for a glass of water, get a frozen pizza out of the freezer to thaw, then saunter back to the living room. I reach for *Playgirl*. The articles are of no interest to me, but I linger over the photo spreads. Now, these images of naked men truly are lovely, the crowning glory of God's creation. My head buzzes as a flow of excited electrons floods my brain. Finally, right there on the couch, I rip off my clothes, and for the first time in the presence of a fully naked man, I take care of business.

Later that evening, after jerking off two more times, I slip *Playgirl* beneath the underwear in my top drawer. I lie in bed understanding for the first time my brother's excitement over his barnyard *Playboy*. Staring into the darkness, I admit to myself that I am a homosexual, but what does that mean?

"Lord," I pray, "can I be a Seventh-day Adventist and a homosexual at the same time?"

June 8, 2013. I'm about to enter an Adventist church located in Greater Vancouver, British Columbia. It's the first time I have worshipped with this congregation. When I step inside the door, the greeter smiles, shakes my hand, and welcomes me with the words, "Happy Sabbath. Are you all alone? You don't have a family?"

"I have two brothers, but they live in Alberta and Ontario," I say.

"Your wife is not with you?" She gives me a pitying look, as though I'm deficient in some way.

"No, I don't have a wife," I say. "I got the gay gene in my family. Right now I don't have a husband either. You don't happen to have a gay brother who's looking for a mate, do you?" She manages a nervous smile, hands me a bulletin outlining the day's service, and turns quickly to the next person. I make my way up to the balcony from where I can make a quick exit if I hear toxic words.

Pastor Kurt looks to be about the age I was when I bought that copy of *Playgirl*. He and his wife and children lead the singing during praise time. Then he begins his sermon. He stands on the people's level instead of high and lifted up in the pulpit. He urges his congregation to make the Church a safe place for all people.

"Why have so many of us made the Church into a gated community?" he asks. "What must Jesus think when he sees us erecting barriers to his house of worship, limiting membership to the privileged few who fit within some narrow, self-righteous dogma?"

He reads the stories about Jesus hanging out with society's outcasts: lepers, the despised Samaritan woman, drunkards, and the woman accused of adultery. He pauses, takes a deep breath, then says, "Sexual orientation, I won't touch with a ten-foot pole, but let me tell you, this remains an opportunity for us to swing open the gates."

I grab my notebook and begin scribbling. "Sexual orientation, I won't touch…" At the same time I'm holding my breath, waiting for him to backtrack, to qualify his statement, to insist that homosexuals can change the bent of their affections, but he doesn't say that. He lets his words sink in, then continues his talk.

His single sentence recognizing that I exist is an extremely cautious statement, but I recognize it as his way of coming out as an LGBT-supportive pastor. After the service I thank him for not condemning me to hellfire, for not holding out the elusive hope that I can change my orientation if I just read my Bible and pray diligently. He reveals that he has read *Torn: Rescuing the Gospel from the Gays-vs.-Christian Debate* by Justin Lee, founder of Gay Christian Network.

"I think this is a very important subject," he says. "I fully realize how hypersensitive people are to the whole issue, so I tread softly. Still, I've been making my views known to others for a number of years now."

"How do people react?" I ask.

"Some people agree with me, but I'm often surprised by others, surprised that they're not further along in their understanding of the issue."

"They need to see the documentary *Seventh-Gay Adventist*," I say.

"I saw it," Kurt says. "I was at the public screening in downtown Vancouver. I even donated to the Kickstarter fund to get it off the ground. I now have my own copy and wish all of our people would watch it." As we conclude our chat, he reaches for my hand and says, "You're more than welcome to worship here and be part of this church."

Driving home, I review the morning's service and my chat with Pastor Kurt. His cautious approach reminds me that coming out is a frightening process not only for LGBT folk but also for those who support them. Church leaders like Pastor Kurt have to be careful with their words and where they speak them. As a gay man, I need to remember that their coming out as gay-supportive clergy can be as difficult a process for them as was my own coming out.

It is now more than thirty years since that cold, winter day in 1984 when Pastor Rickson demanded my keys, but my coming out story did not end there. I continue to come out: again...and again...and again. Each time I tell the truth about myself, I pray that my honesty will chip away at the brittle wall of lies that centuries of one-sided theology have built. By coming out, I hope to encourage positive attitudes among clergy and congregations alike, so that one day all Seventh-day Adventist churches will fling wide their gates to welcome God's queer tribe.

Living La Vida Media

Reid Vanderburgh

I WAS THIRTY-NINE YEARS OLD, LIVING AS A LESBIAN, WHEN I FIRST realized I'd probably be happier living as a guy. I did not take kindly to this realization, for several reasons. First, I had quite a life built up in the Portland, Oregon, lesbian community. I had been a founding member of the Portland Lesbian Choir for nine years standing, and leaving that group was not on my horizon.

Second, I had a family of choice with whom my bonds were stronger than those with my biological family. All were lesbians. All were fellow choir members, or members of my mixed chorus, Bridges Vocal Ensemble. Or members of both. Queer folks find family as we are able, and often the bonds forged through living in a hostile society are stronger than the bonds of blood connection. I was scared of my realization—if I became a man, would I lose my family of choice?

Finally, I had a negative reaction to the idea of being trans because I had absorbed the mainstream belief that being trans was weird, sick, and perverted. Whenever I did see someone obviously trans, I felt uneasy and off balance, as if I was in the presence of someone who was psychotic, or not fully human. I had some vague equation of the terms *transsexual* and *drag queen* being synonymous, which of course had made it impossible for me to recognize myself as a transsexual earlier in my life. I've loathed feminine clothing for as long as I can remember, which is hardly the attitude of a drag queen!

I'd never had conscious fantasies about being male. I had just never felt completely at home in my skin as a female, causing a low-grade anxiety and depression that was growing steadily as I aged. I hated women's bathrooms. I did not like introducing myself to others, as my former name was highly feminine. I avoided describing myself as a lesbian and felt vaguely uncomfortable referring to myself as a woman. I had never visited an ob-gyn in my life. I was full of contradictions and felt an enigma to myself—not an easy life for a Virgo.

I would probably still be living in denial had my then-partner not come out to me in the spring of 1995, telling me one night, "I've always felt like a man inside." This effectively held a mirror to my soul. I could no longer ignore what I saw there, but I was not prepared to face it. The effect was rather like a badly done substance abuse intervention. Because of the negative attitudes I'd internalized about what it meant to be trans, I had a difficult time feeling okay about the concept of going through female-to-male transition.

Then one day a bisexual friend said to me, with some envy in her voice, "What a gift, to be able to live as both sexes in one lifetime." This one phrase reframed the experience for me, for the first time putting a positive spin on the concept of being trans. Nowhere else had I encountered a positive interpretation of what it might mean to be trans. I moved forward with a great deal more confidence and excitement at the possibilities inherent in the unexpected opportunity life had presented me.

I postponed my physical transition for nearly two years, waiting for the Portland Lesbian Choir to record its first CD. I spent those two years in gender limbo-land, being seen primarily as male in my undergrad classes at Portland State University (unless I opened my mouth to speak), being seen as in transition at work, and being seen as a lesbian during choir rehearsals. I felt the split keenly, never being able to quite integrate these various aspects of my life into one cohesive whole, despite the fact that I had come out to everyone who was important to me. Transition cannot be done in the closet.

Once I began hormones and had top surgery, life became much simpler as my former lesbian life faded away gradually. However, what I found is that I did not become more male in my outlook on life. I became fully male in appearance while retaining many of the values I'd learned in the lesbian community. I did not feel much more comfortable calling myself a man than I had calling myself a woman, or a lesbian, though I felt fine calling myself a guy and definitely felt more comfortable in my own skin. I did not lose my lesbian family of choice, though I did lose my place within the lesbian community—that's not my tribe any longer.

I gradually came to realize that I had not transitioned from female to male. I had transitioned from female to not-female. In the ensuing years, I have come to agree with Kate Bornstein, a trans woman writer and performer, who stated, "I know I'm not a man—about that much I'm very clear, and I've come to the conclusion that I'm probably not a woman, either."

I wasn't raised to be a man. I did not absorb male socialization. I did not have testosterone dominant in my body, with the resulting imperious sex drive, until I was forty-one years old. I have never thought of women as other than my equal and don't believe I can. I don't have any of the traditional attitudes considered male in this society. While I am *capable* of having a monotone discussion about sports, I'd *rather* have a passionate conversation about life.

I've become increasingly convinced, both through personal experience and through conversations with other trans people, that it's not really possible to transition fully from one sex to another. Cisgender men see me as a man, though they quickly come to realize there's something not quite man-like about me. Many assume this must mean I'm gay, as the thought never enters their minds that perhaps I am a trans man.

Cisgender women see me as a man, though they quickly come to realize there's something not quite man-like about me. I've had a number of cis women comment with surprise on how comfortable they feel with me. Many of them, unaware that I'm trans, assume this must mean

I'm gay. I've never yet met a cis man or cis woman who has figured out on their own that I was assigned female at birth.

Now, I feel I'm neither man nor woman, though the limitations of English force me to choose sides, if only so I may have terminology with which to describe myself. So, I'm a guy, much more comfortable with male pronouns than female, but not really feeling like "a man." I'm living *la vida media*—life in the middle. I have not crossed the bridge from "female" on one side, over an immeasurable chasm, to become "male" on the other side. Rather, I have *become* the bridge.

Cellophane

Joseph A. Shapiro

Todd and I inch our way through the crowd of folks who have also waited in line to gain entry to Marie's Crisis this evening. It's Saturday night, and the place is packed with people who've come to sing. I'm surprised once again by the increasing number of straight young couples among the gay men who frequent this place. Marie's patrons seem far more mixed each time I visit—much more so than when I first came here, as a married man, sixteen years ago.

Marie's is a West Village piano bar that has served the gay community in its well-worn location since the 1890s. On the far wall hangs a faded and yellowed antique mirror etched with images of battle scenes from both the American and French Revolutionary Wars. It always reminds me of that other revolution that took place only a block from here during the early-morning hours of June 28, 1969, at the Stonewall Inn. The movement for gay rights in America began that night, when the New York City police took their harassment of homosexuals in gay-identified establishments one step too far.

Not long ago Marie's was almost exclusively frequented by homosexual musical theater queens who came to feed their craving for show tunes. There are also men who come here mainly to cruise for other like-minded guys: some dreaming of a newfound relationship, others on the prowl for a one-night stand. I've been both. I've seen all kinds of people here over the years—and I've kissed more than a few. But this evening is for Todd and me. For us.

Folks crowd around the upright piano boxed in by a Formica bar top and against the much longer bar running along the far end of this deep, rectangular room, whose wood-beamed ceilings are rimmed with Christmas lights all year long. The exuberant energy is so strong that I can feel the resulting vibrations in the old wooden-plank floor. They're singing a medley of tunes from the Kander and Ebb musical, *Chicago*:

> *Cellophane*
> *Mister Cellophane*
> *Should have been my name*
> *Mister Cellophane*
> *'Cause you can look right through me*
> *Walk right by me*
> *And never know I'm there…*

I never come into this room without hearing a lyric that brings me back into my own life, that speaks to my own issues. Maybe that's what musical theater is all about. Or what it's about for me, anyway. So tonight I'm "Mister Cellophane" again, and I recall all the years of my life when those closest to me walked right by me without ever knowing the homosexual child, and later adult, inside—seeing only the boy, and then the straight-acting man, whom I chose to project. I wonder how much longer I'll be immersed in this painful struggle to understand how and why I felt the need to hide that "me." Then again, might it have been others who simply insisted on my invisibility?

We're working our way through the crowd now, edging slowly toward the far corner of the piano, where we see just enough space for the two of us to stand behind a youngish straight couple, perhaps in their early thirties. They're perched on stools to the right of Dan Daly, this evening's pianist and master of ceremonies. Dan is a slender man, with short-cropped brown hair, in his midforties. He looks pleased: his clear-glass tip bowl, large enough for a family of goldfish, has just returned to the piano top filled with dollar bills after being passed among the patrons.

He starts to play, and I start to sing along. For the moment it doesn't matter if there's anyone else in the room. As it always has, singing transports me to a secret place where I can begin to understand who I am and what my life is all about. In so many ways, the song he's now playing, "Where Is Love?" from *Oliver!* is a theme song for me. I first listened to it on a vinyl album with my childhood friend, Carl Brown, more than fifty years ago. We sang the song together, but Carl had the courage to answer the question, where is love? long before I even dared to think about it. He came out of the closet about the same time that I stepped into it. He followed his dream to live a life that felt natural and right to him, as I ran away from mine. I'll never stop wondering what might have been if we'd followed that dream together.

Setting thoughts of Carl aside, I smile at Todd. He is a sweet, gentle person—the kind of man who always asks what he can do to make my life easier, more comfortable. We share a love of music and singing, and that's what brings us here tonight.

Dan Daly plays the introduction to "Do-Re-Mi": "Let's start at the very beginning…" A fellow on the other side of the room calls out, "What song is this?" I can't help myself: I blurt out, equally loudly, "Who let *straight* people in here?" Chuckles abound. The young man in front of me, the one sitting with a woman close to his age, turns around, cracking up with laughter, extends his hand toward me, and says, "I *love* your style." And he winks at me. I smile in return. Am I smiling at him? Or at myself, transported back in time, about sixteen years, sitting in this very room, next to *my* wife?

For the next two hours or so the songs, and the drinking, continue. Todd and I know most, but by no means all, of the lyrics. This charming young man in front of me knows all of the words. He's short in stature, with curly, dusty-blond hair and gold wire-rimmed glasses, and in his tight-fitting, V-necked black tee he looks more like the young gay men in the room than their straight, more conservatively dressed counterparts. His black jeans are equally tight, and I'm curious about what we'll see when he stands up. I wonder if his companion realizes who he resembles this evening. She wears a large diamond ring. Assuming it came from him, I can't help but wonder if it was his effort to purchase her happiness and contentment, for I've already decided that he and I have a lot more than our love of show tunes in common.

Should I tell him that kind of appeasement only works for so long?

She sings quietly along with a few of the songs but seems more interested in drinking and texting and checking her watch. She appears to be wishing that she were someplace else. And who can blame her? But she isn't someplace else. She's here, sitting next to him. And almost never looking at him. *She* must *be his wife*, I think. If she were his fag hag, she'd be conversing with him and having fun.

He, on the other hand, cannot turn around frequently enough to share his enjoyment of the music with me and Todd. And I'm enjoying our unspoken camaraderie.

Seeing how unhappy his "wife" looks makes me wonder why she agreed to come to a gay bar with him in the first place. Could it be that she didn't know what Marie's was? Or does she suspect something and want to keep her eye on him? To this day my ex-wife claims that she never had a clue that I was gay. But then I never took her to a gay bar…at least not until after I came out to her.

The young woman's increasing impatience begins to wear on her companion, and as the evening progresses, it seems more and more difficult for him to remain animated and joyful as he sings along with us and the rest of the boisterous crowd at Marie's. But he doesn't stop turning to look at us. Actually, it now feels like he's looking at me. As if he knows something more about me, or knows there is something more that I might understand about him. I think I detect a pleading expression on his face. His eyes are glazing over. Or is this all in my imagination? Projected feelings, memories, anxiety from my past; it was, after all, to this same spot in late 1995 that I brought my wife, in a misguided mission to introduce her to what I had finally come to accept as my new way of life.

It was 1996, sixteen years ago, and I held the door to Marie's Crisis open for Lisa as music wafted from below. With a pained expression that seemed both hesitant and determined, she followed me down the stairs.

This was our third visit to a gay establishment since I'd announced to her, after eighteen years of marriage, that I was gay. I was both relieved and horrified when Lisa proclaimed that we'd find a way to continue making our marriage work. When I imagined coming out to my wife, the script always ended with her throwing me out of the house in what would be a scene of both devastation and liberation. I was trying to be clear that I felt a continuation of our marriage to be an improbable outcome. But having been with Lisa as friend, boyfriend, and husband since high school—twenty-five years of our lives—I felt, I knew, that I owed it to her to ease her into whatever transition was before us, and to help her understand why it was happening. She needed to know that for me, being gay wasn't just a question of with whom someone has sex. It was being part of a different culture, a unique awareness, a way of life. It was, for me, feeling more at home in a piano bar than at a ballpark. It was watching *Will & Grace* and relating mostly to Jack. It was that the Tony Awards were a highlight of my year, and I couldn't care less who was playing in the Super Bowl. And mostly for me it was a matter of whom and how I love. I hoped that these field trips would give Lisa that understanding as well—for my own peace of mind, if not hers.

And so we agreed that I would take her to some of the places where I felt I could be myself. I believed that her agenda was to demonstrate her ability and willingness to share my new "interests," as she labeled them. To show me how flexible and understanding she was willing to be. It was an extraordinary effort on her part, with a goal of keeping our eighteen-year marriage intact. She believed—I suppose she needed to believe—that this was my version of a midlife crisis, and that if she waited it out, if she could survive it, I'd eventually come back to my senses and our marriage would resume its normal course.

But the thought of remaining in our marriage was terrifying to me. I was deeply hurt that she would question my integrity, as she did when she dismissed my coming out to her—the ultimate confession of my truth—as a phase that I'd soon get over. At the same time, I knew she must love me very much to put herself through an experience as difficult and painful as this. Perhaps a profound sense of guilt was driving me, and I felt that I had no choice but to indulge her request to experience the gay life to which I was drawn.

And so there we were, an hour and a half from our suburban home, at a gay piano bar in the West Village. We sat together at one of the few small wooden tables. It was early evening, and the place was sparsely populated. The fellow behind the piano asked if there was something we'd like to hear, and I suggested a song from *A Chorus Line*, a musical that Lisa and I had enjoyed together.

As he began to play, Maggie Wirth, the singing cocktail waitress I'd known since her days at Eighty Eights—another piano bar—came over to take our drink order. I asked for a vodka tonic, and Lisa requested a Coke. Minutes later Maggie returned with our drinks in glass tumblers.

As I paid Maggie for the drinks, adding a generous tip, Lisa glared at me. "I'm not drinking that! I thought they would come in plastic cups. Who knows who drank from that glass last or what disease they might have!"

I was aghast that she could even think such a thing, let alone say it—and I felt the blood rushing to my face. Perhaps it was at that moment I truly realized the futility of trying to bring our very different worlds together. My mind flashed back to a discussion we'd had when Lisa was pregnant for the third time. It was 1986, and she was working as a registered nurse. The AIDS crisis had found its way to New Jersey, and she was terrified of sticking herself with a needle and contracting HIV. She no longer felt secure that her double gowns, her surgical mask, or her multiple latex gloves would protect her health and that of our unborn child. And so we agreed that she'd stop working as a hospital nurse and consider other, safer ways to contribute to our income, both during and after that pregnancy.

Now I sat red-faced in Marie's knowing that there was no connection between what had once been Lisa's legitimate anxiety about contact with HIV-contaminated blood and her baseless fear of using a drinking glass that may have been previously used by an HIV-positive man. I also knew that there would be no convincing her of that.

"Let's go," I said, and stood and walked toward the door.

The young woman who reminds me tonight so much of Lisa, still sitting at the bar and ignoring the young man who reminds me so much of myself, stands, twisting a handful of her straight blonde hair with her right hand, and works her way back through the crowd toward the stairs that lead down to the basement restrooms. Her young man puts his head down on his crossed arms on the bar. I can see that his eyes are open and he's staring down at the dark tile floor. He remains in that position for quite a while. When he hears her return, he leans over the bar, puts a few dollars more into Dan's tip bowl, and tells her that he's ready to leave. She wears a look of relief as she heads toward the exit.

He wishes us a good evening. He looks so resigned.

"Hey, guy," I say to him, now looking directly into his eyes. "Why don't you just come out already?"

He smiles then and winks at me once more, as if to say, "I knew you'd understand."

As he walks away, I put my arm around the back of Todd's slender waist and reach up to kiss his bearded face.

Why don't you just come out? It's the question I've asked myself for as many years as I can remember. Todd and I have been dating for only six months, but he's heard enough of my stories to understand that the pain of my coming out as a then-married father of three remains as real for me now as the moment it began. It's a feeling of loss that can't be resolved, for I could and would never wish my children away.

Nothing is more important to me than my love for them. Yet I'll never know how I might have responded if someone earlier in my lifetime had asked me, "Why don't you just come out?"

Perhaps I would not have lived so much of my life caught between two worlds.

"I think I'm ready to leave now," I say to Todd. "It's been a long evening."

And then the crowd starts singing a song from *The Wiz*. We sing along as we work our way to the door. "Believe in yourself, right from the start. You'll have brains. You'll have a heart. You'll have courage to last your whole life through. If you believe in yourself as I believe in you…"

And I surprise myself as I begin to cry.

Contributor Bios

Patrick Cornelius is originally from the East Coast, outside of Philadelphia. After spending over twenty years working in disability services, the last twelve in elite paralympic sport, he decided to follow his dream of becoming a mortician. Now licensed as a funeral director and embalmer in the state of Oregon, Patrick enjoys working in the Columbia River Gorge serving families and the community. He also enjoys running, working out, and the beautiful outdoors.

William Dameron is a prolific blogger at *The Huffington Post, The Good Men Project,* and his personal blog, *The Authentic Life.* He has published essays in *The Boston Globe, Saranac Review,* and *5x5.* He has won Blogher's Voices of the Year award for the past three years and has completed a memoir manuscript. He lives in Boston with his husband.

Clayton Delery-Edwards is the author of *The Up Stairs Lounge Arson: Thirty-Two Deaths in a New Orleans Gay Bar, June 24, 1973* (McFarland Publishing, 2014). He taught English at the Louisiana School for Math, Science, and the Arts in Natchitoches from 1989 to 2015. He married his husband, Aaron, in a Canadian ceremony in 2008. Clayton has recently retired from teaching. He and his husband now live in New Orleans.

David R. Gillespie is an author, hospice volunteer coordinator, and instructor in religion and philosophy for Furman University's OLLI program. He has been publishing since 1974 (way before his coming out); his first short story was published in 2000. One year after his front-page coming out, he entered into what has been his longest relationship with the love of his life. When he is not coordinating volunteers, teaching, or writing and reading, he most likely can be found on his boat enjoying lake life with his husband. He wishes he could have had just one more conversation with his late father.

Wayne Gregory, author of the memoir *The Tongues of Men and Angels*, is a graduate of the Attic Atheneum and a former Hawthorne Fellow. His work has appeared in *The Sun*, *Alltopia*, *Ashe Journal*, *The Hawthorne*, and the Lambda award-winning anthology *Portland Queer*. He is a linguist and a faculty member at Portland State University and also teaches creative writing at the Attic Institute. Wayne is a proud father and grandfather and a card-carrying member of the Portland Gay Men's Chorus. Originally from Louisiana, he now lives in Portland, Oregon.

Andrew L. Huerta lives in Tucson, Arizona, where he has spent the past fifteen years in higher education teaching and advising students who are the first in their families to attend college. After completing his MA in creative writing and PhD in education, he is now in the process of completing his first two works of fiction: a collection of short stories entitled *A Different Man*, and a novel entitled *Raggedy Anthony*. His short stories have appeared in such publications as *Chelsea Station Magazine*, *The Round Up Writer's Zine: Pride Edition*, *Creating Iris*, *Jonathan*, and *The Storyteller*. For more information, please visit www.andrewlhuerta.com.

Anil Kamal is a public servant for the federal government. He recently completed his MFA in Creative Writing from the University of British Columbia. His thesis, a television series entitled *Saffron*, about a lawyer seeking a midcareer switch to drag queen extraordinaire, is currently seeking production. Originally from Ottawa, he now lives in Toronto, Ontario, with his partner and their six-year-old pug, Kala.

David B. Livingstone is a freelance writer, corporate communications consultant, and occasional punk rock guitarist living and working in suburban Detroit, Michigan. He has written arts and entertainment criticism for a variety of newspapers and magazines in the United States and United Kingdom. He recently contributed to *Recognize: The Voices of Bisexual Men*, an anthology of bi men's writing published by the Bisexual Resource Center.

David Meischen writes poetry and fiction. His work has appeared in *Copper Nickel, The Southern Review, Salamander, Bellingham Review, Southern Poetry Review*, and elsewhere. "Crossing the Nueces" is part of a memoir, currently in progress; another excerpt appeared in *The Gettysburg Review*. Meischen has a novel in stories, currently with an enthusiastic agent. He won the Writers' League of Texas Manuscript Contest in Mainstream Fiction, 2011, and the Talking Writing Fiction Contest, 2012. Cofounder and managing editor of Dos Gatos Press, a nonprofit dedicated to poets and poetry, he lives in Albuquerque, New Mexico, with his husband—also his copublisher and co-editor—Scott Wiggerman.

Samuel Peterson is a fifty-plus-year-old trans guy, performer, writer, and activist. His book, *Trunky (transgender junky), A Memoir of Institutionalization and Southern Hospitality*, will be published by Transgress Press fall 2016, while his one-person play, *F to M to Octopus*, is currently seeking production. You can find him in Kate Bornstein and S. Bear Bergman's cutting-edge anthology, *Gender Outlaws: The Next Generation*, and online at www.samuelpeterson.org. Or where he is now, in bed with his cats.

Robert L. Ramsay grew up on a farm on the Canadian prairies. He earned his teaching credentials from Brandon University and a bachelor of arts from the University of Winnipeg. After teaching for twenty years in Manitoba, he moved to Victoria, British Columbia, where he worked in municipal government administration for thirteen years. He now lives in Surrey, British Columbia. He studied creative writing at the University of Winnipeg, Camosun College, in Victoria and North Island College in Courtenay. His first nonfiction article, on interior design, was published in 1971. Since then he has published nonfiction articles in magazines such as *Senior Living, Exercise for Men Only, The American Organist*, and *Christian Single*. In the mideighties he wrote stories for *Honcho, Mandate*, and *Playguy*. Now he is once again writing fiction. Most recently, his story "Helen and Gerry" appeared in *Off the Rocks*.

Joseph Schreiber is a writer, critic, and photographer living in Calgary, Alberta. He is a contributor at *Numéro Cinq* magazine. His reviews have also appeared in other literary journals including *3:AM Magazine* and *The Scofield*. Presently he is working on an experimental prose project exploring the realities of living as a gay transgender man.

Joseph A. Shapiro teaches writing and Transgender Literature at Hunter College in New York City. He has an MFA in creative writing from Hunter College and was a 2010 Lambda Literary Fellow. "Cellophane" is an excerpt from his forthcoming memoir by the same title. It was first published in *Cactus Heart Literary Journal* in 2014.

Reid Vanderburgh is a retired therapist living in Portland, Oregon, who now focuses on writing and teaching. He teaches continuing education classes on issues pertaining to LGBTQ identity and various aspects of the transition process. He is on the board of both PFLAG Portland and his local GSA Youth Chorus. He also sings in the Portland Gay Men's Chorus, and in recent years he has provided workshops for various gay and lesbian choruses regarding trans inclusivity. He is the author of two books: *Transition and Beyond: Observations on Gender Identity* and *Journeys of Transformation: Stories from Across the Acronym.*

Jean-Pierre Vidrine was born in the small town of Ville Platte, Louisiana. He graduated from Louisiana State University with a degree in journalism…just months after discovering that he hated journalism. For a time he was a comic book reviewer for *Another Castle.* He is also a sometime contributor to the blog *Divergent Lifestyles.* He now lives in Chicago with his spouse and cat.

Van Waffle is a Canadian journalist. He lives in Waterloo, Ontario, with Danny Ouellette, his partner of thirteen years. He blogs about urban nature at www.vanwaffle.com.

About the Editor

Vinnie Kinsella lives in the famously weird city of Portland, Oregon. He works as a writer, editor, book designer, publishing consultant, and workshop presenter. After coming out as gay at thirty-four years old, he founded the PDX Late Bloomers Club, a social-support organization for men who came out later in life. Drawing from this experience, he has developed a passion for supporting those entering into the LGBTQ community at an older age and educating those who serve as their allies. Vinnie can often be seen performing with the Portland Gay Men's Chorus or reading a book in one of Portland's numerous coffee shops. More information about his work can be found at vinniekinsella.com.

A Note about Resources

Coming out is a challenge best taken on with support. To help, we have provided at list of resources on our website for both those coming out and their loved ones. This includes links to organizations, recommendation for other books, and tips on how to start your own Late Bloomers Club. You access these resources at fashionablylatebook.com/resources.

CPSIA information can be obtained
at www.ICGtesting.com
Printed in the USA
LVOW11s1641291116

514956LV00003B/637/P

9 780997 749106